D1544063

Great Cartoonists
AND THEIR ART

Franklin Booth; reprinted from collection of Art Wood

Great Cartoonists

AND THEIR ART

By *Art Wood*

PELICAN PUBLISHING COMPANY

GRETNA 1987

Library of Congress Cataloging-in-Publication Data

Wood, Art, 1927–
    Great cartoonists.

    1. Wood, Art, 1927-   2. Cartoonists—United
States—Biography. 3. Caricatures and cartoons—United
States. 4. Cartoonists—United States—Biography—
History and criticism. 5. United States—Politics and
government—Caricatures and cartoons. I. Title.
NC1429.W598A2   1987   741.5'092'4 [B]   87-2412
ISBN: 0-88289-476-5

Manufactured in the United States of America
Published by Pelican Publishing Company, Inc.
1101 Monroe Street, Gretna, Louisiana 70053

Designed by Karen H. Foval

Contents

Introduction

THE AUTHOR is a nationally known editor and cartoonist with over 35 years of newspaper experience, having won numerous journalistic and governmental awards. His work has been reprinted in major publications in America and abroad. He has been active in the National Cartoonists Society as a member since 1948 and is a founding father of the Association of American Editorial Cartoonists, having served on the Board since the 1950s and president of the group in 1975.

Starting at the age of 12, he began acquiring the best original work of the nation's graphic artists until today the collection is one of the largest and most representative in the world, including the work of over 2,000 artists and over 30,000 pieces of art—from the size of a postcard to the expanse of a wall. The collection encompasses caricature, the political cartoon, comic drawings, animation, and illustration. Selected original drawings serve as illustrations for this book.

The book approaches cartooning at a number of levels. While autobiographical in structure, it also tells how other cartoonists think, work, and create. It does this by focusing on notable practitioners past and present, all of whom have been close friends of the author. These artists give an insight into their working habits, and the book is spiced with humorous anecdotes.

In addition, the author relates how he built such a large collection of drawings that have been displayed in major galleries and museums in the United States and overseas.

The book also gives an inside look at political leaders whom the author has known, studied at close range, and drawn since the 1940s, including Franklin Roosevelt, Harry Truman, Dwight D. Eisenhower, John Kennedy, Richard Nixon, Jerry Ford, Jimmy Carter, and Ronald Reagan.

Great Cartoonists

AND THEIR ART

1

In the Beginning

WHERE does one begin? Salvador Dali recalls and recounts pre-existence in the womb. Fortunately, my memory does not go back that far!

My first impressions were happy ones focused on a small town in western Virginia. Both my parents were born in Virginia. My father, of English stock, was from the tobacco town of Petersburg, well-known during the War Between the States as a trading center, and famous for "the Battle of the Crater." My mother was from the other end of the state, the lovely little city of Lynchburg, nestled in the Blue Ridge Mountains. Lynchburg had many famous residents, foremost of whom was Carter Glass, who held numerous federal posts, including that of secretary of the treasury under Woodrow Wilson.

Lynchburg, like Rome, was built on seven hills. My family lived on College Hill at the top of a steep cobblestone incline named for the noted Virginia general who stood, in contrast to the street, as straight as a stone wall. Jackson Street was a gracious address in those days, boasting large tree-shaded homes. Many were colonial in architecture, but most were Victorian with generous doses of gingerbread. Prominent were the large front and side porches where neighbors gathered to gossip and share recipes. It was a relaxed atmosphere, typical of the South.

As a child, everything seemed so BIG. Books and bicycles, trees and houses, pets and people took on gigantic proportions. It was frightening and frustrating to be unable to see over the top of the bureau. It was even more embarrassing to have to call for help to reach a comb on a cabinet or a lemon drop hidden in a jar on a high ledge.

The largest dwelling of all was a white clapboard house at 1020 Jackson Street. To me it was home—the most beautiful structure in the world. With gingerbread carvings and blood-red tin roof, the columned house meandered over the better part of a city block. A wide avenue ran past the side yard, and streetcars strained to make the steep grade.

Streetcars were not the only vehicles that found it difficult to climb Lynchburg's cobblestone thoroughfares. On wet mornings, or when the pavements had just been washed down, horse-drawn ice wagons were known to slide precariously downhill. The pawing of horses, the sparks from clashing hoofs, and the loud grating sound as brakes were applied signaled that free ice was on the way. For in all the confusion, large chips of ice fell from the open cart like hail in a summer storm. The children in Pied Piper-style would follow the cart, and the iceman would return up the hill with a much lighter load.

The barny old house at the top of Jackson

Street was a child's delight. The halls were spacious and the rooms immense. Large fireplaces stretched out in every room, and recessed closets were perfect for hiding or for secret club meetings. The pantry contained cookies of every variety, and the huge kitchen was a wonderland of cabinets and machinery. The yard was no less intriguing, with heavy shrubs and numerous flower plots. Beds of yellow and purple pansies hugged the ground. Roses in shades of red reached upward to the pillars of the porch. Standing guard over the garden were towering hollyhocks in a rainbow of color. Statuesque oak trees also stood straight like soldiers in parade dress. The tree roots spread far into the ground like shadowy shapes of sea serpents skimming through a dark green sea. It was a perfect playground, and hours were spent outside roughhousing until exhaustion forced us inside.

As an active ten-year-old, I objected strenuously to an afternoon nap but secretly enjoyed coming into the library to pore over the large selection of books that lined the walls. As long as I was quiet, no one in the family objected. Although the stories themselves were exciting, the main attractions for me were the illustrations. Howard Pyle's *King Arthur,* N. C. Wyeth's *Treasure Island,* and Frank Schoonover's *Robinson Crusoe* were to me living volumes. I studied them until the pages were spotted with fingerprints and the drawings worn thin.

Pyle, Wyeth, and Schoonover specialized in drawing knights in gleaming armor and pirates with ragged beards and spotted eyepatches. You could feel the villains' hot breath on your neck and see them leaping from the page to dance along the bottom of your bed. This was an exciting diet for an adventure-hungry kid.

Howard Pyle's characters were delicately drawn and historically correct in costume and attire, but his figures seemed stiff to me as a young reader and his people had an unexplainable sour look. Perhaps his characters were *too* fearsome, frightening, and realistic. I leaned more to the work of John Gruelle, who later achieved fame and fortune for his creations of Raggedy Ann and Raggedy Andy.

A special favorite was *Grimm's Fairy Tales* illustrated by Gruelle. Many of his chapter illustrations were rendered in pen and ink and scattered throughout the text, but the frontispiece and six or seven plates were printed in full color. Gruelle's characterizations of giants and elves were scary, and his eerie sketches of witches and monsters brought the stories to life. To pass the time, I copied his illustrations and attempted to enlarge them for display in my bedroom. My efforts were feeble, and I was discouraged when my awkward drawings did not resemble those in the book. Drawing was difficult, but I persisted.

I sought out two artists in the neighborhood who took an interest in my early sketches and gave me encouragement and help. The first, Mrs. Schaeffer, was white-haired and elderly, not at all my picture of an artist. She was a lifetime resident of the city but still spoke with a slight German accent. Her home was small but attractive, and I recall the dull, rust-colored brick that contrasted with the bright hollyhocks engulfing the house. She loved flowers, and her paintings were always of flower arrangements or gardens. I tried flower studies, but floral arrangements and leaf patterns bored a ten-year-old boy.

Almost directly across the street from Mrs. Schaeffer's flower garden was a house that stood high above the street. The doorway seemed miles from the level of the yard and could be reached only by climbing a massive set of granite steps. These quarry stones, piled one above the other, made it difficult for a youngster to climb without carefully pacing himself so as not to be out of breath when he pushed the doorbell. It was also difficult for the other neighborhood artist who lived there. Elizabeth Crowe was an invalid. She had been crippled by polio in her youth and had to be trained to walk again. She moved slowly and with great difficulty, but was so cheerful that the disability was overlooked. The imposing brick house with the steep, hewn steps was home for Elizabeth, her elderly mother, and her brother, Walter—who was a designer and architect.

Elizabeth had a strong face despite her thin, almost tubercular, figure. A wisp of a person, she seemed to hover in mid-air. She inspected each visitor with a studied eye and thickish glasses. Shy, soft-spoken, and reticent, she bubbled with enthusiasm when the conversation turned to art. She was a talented painter, and her large colorful canvasses filled the huge walls of the old mansion.

Elizabeth loved the outdoors, probably because she had spent so many years confined to a hospital bed or restricted to her room. Her vivid pictures of the Blue Ridge showed this devotion to nature. The many-hued mountains in broad brush strokes spoke as eloquently of God's glory as the Good Book. The designs of her paintings were carefully conceived and, although painstakingly rendered, gave an impression of ease and rapidity. I greatly admired her work and would sit for hours listening to her discuss technique and design. She explained step by step how she had gone about each painting, from thumbnail sketch to the completed canvas. It was a learning experience that I relished and continued to do so throughout my career, sitting at the feet of many noted artists absorbing pointers and picking up valuable information.

I can still see her lovely canvas of a gigantic mill with water rushing down the sluice. Intrigued and excited by her paintings, I decided to try one myself.

Until this time all my sketches had been in pencil on lined composition paper or brown paper bags that filled the kitchen closet. A trip to the Five and Ten provided a cheap watercolor set, and I recall the deep disappointment of my first effort. The flaccid brush that came with the inexpensive set was not suited to rapid placement of color, and what I thought would be a pleasant pastime became an arduous task. The color would dry before the watercolor could be blended, and the dry-brush technique that resulted was not at all what I had envisioned. To any artist, young or old, this is the ultimate frustration: You see mentally what you want to portray on paper, but the drawing fails to capture the vision. This is the reason so many young artists give up. But I was determined that one day my finished product would resemble one of the lovely paintings that Elizabeth Crowe seemed to produce with such ease and proficiency or would imitate the imaginative illustrations of a John Gruelle. Time would tell.

2

The Roosevelt Years

MY FATHER was offered a legal position in Washington, D.C., and we arrived on the outskirts of the nation's capital in the heat of summer at dusk, having meandered through the Shenandoah Valley hills and over narrow two-lane roads. We often moved at a snail's pace behind slow-moving farm vehicles. The countryside was dark as we approached Memorial Bridge. Although we were tired, our eyes sparkled as we crossed the river, for the city seemed afire with light. We were unsure of the way to our destination on Connecticut Avenue and headed downtown. It was a pleasant mistake. We passed the columned Lincoln Memorial, approached the George Washington Monument bathed in light, and circled the ellipse by the White House. Eventually we turned from 16th Street onto Connecticut Avenue where my parents had rented an apartment. It was exciting to view the architecture and the setting and then to realise that we were in such an historic city. I still get a thrill every time I fly into the City of Lights and view the impressive skyline from above.

The reason we were moving to Washington was Carter Glass. At the time, he was the senior senator from Virginia. He had from childhood been a living legend. During the Civil War, as a mere lad, he had saved his hometown of Lynchburg from certain destruc-

tion by taking a toy gun and positioning himself on the bridge at the James River leading into town to challenge the oncoming Northern troops.

"You cannot burn my city," the lad cried, as he blocked the Yankee horsemen. "I won't let you."

Impressed by his audacity and courage, the Union Officer lifted him onto his horse, and rode into the city of Seven Hills. Not a hand was laid on the small Virginia town by the Federal army. Carter Glass became secretary of the treasury under Woodrow Wilson. He later resigned to accept the post of U.S. senator, where he served for over a quarter of a century. He was president pro-tem of the Senate and chairman of the powerful Senate Appropriations Committee, and was one of the more formidable statesmen in Washington.

My grandfather, Frank Jennings, who died at an early age, had served as Glass's campaign manager. In contrast, Glass lived to be almost 100. The senator was very fond of my mother, whom he had known since she was a girl. When a legal position developed in one of the federal agencies, Senator Glass brought my father, who was an attorney, to Washington.

The capital city was less security-minded in those days. This was before the Puerto Rican shoot-out in front of Blair House and the similar debacle in the Senate. I recall going with Senator Glass onto the floor of the Senate where I would sit in his lap as he peeled an apple, a Virginia product, and read *his* paper (literally), since he owned the *Lynchburg News*. It was also a thrill from such a vantage point to see close up the sartorial splendor of Sen. Clyde Hooie, who always wore a black coat, string tie, and striped pants, or to watch the frazzled, perspiring Sam Rayburn as he made his rounds in the House chamber. Senator Glass was a tender-hearted man, fond of children and particularly gracious to me because of my mother. He was very different on the telephone, however. The senator hated to talk on the phone and even tried (unsuccessfully) to ban telephones from the Senate. Several times I called to thank him for a present and he growled into the receiver. You often were not sure whether he was on the line or not. After his secretary put him on the line, he would say, "Eh!" and there would be a long, terrifying pause. You had to do the talking, only it was like talking to yourself. At the end of such a one-sided conversation, he would say, "Very well," and hang up. I was hurt until I learned he treated everyone in the same manner. This up-front view of Washington was heady stuff for a small-town boy. Excitement and fun were wrapped together like colored string and Christmas paper.

In pre-World War II America, Roosevelt was "God." He had charisma, a hypnotic voice and a brash, sparkling personality. He could do no wrong. Herbert Hoover was the "devil" and Roosevelt the "savior." Seldom in the history of our country has a man been so elevated, so revered, and so loved. There were detractors such as columnist Westbrook Pegler and other critics, including Carter Glass, but Roosevelt was the popular hero despite the crippling physical disability of polio. He sympathized with the common man despite his aristocratic name and background.

In my younger years, Roosevelt was all we knew. He was the consummate politician. My father was a Democrat, and when the president called the nation to order with a fire-side chat, we all dutifully gathered around the radio. Roosevelt's resilient voice, distinctive and strong, was the backbone of public confidence.

Living in Washington, everyone wanted to see the great man in person. Parades were the usual outlet for public adulation, and Roosevelt was as fine an actor as he was a speaker. Waving at the crowds with a swing of the hand or a flick of his tapered cigarette holder, the president possessed the original toothpaste smile. Whenever world dignitaries or royalty visited America, the Roosevelts threw a picnic or a parade. Ziegfeld would have been proud of these performances. In the damp cold of winter or during the humid, sticky Washington summers, crowds would stand three deep along the parade route to see the president and his tall first lady with her judicial outfits and protruding teeth.

During the 1938 visit of King George VI and Queen Mary of Great Britain, the *Washington Post* had carefully traced the route that the presidential party would take, and we positioned ourselves near the British Embassy on Massachusetts Avenues, not far from Rock Creek Bridge. It was cold and raw, and the wind was pelting us with dead leaves and dust. We sat on the curb bundled up with comforters and army blankets. As is often the case with politicians, the parade was delayed. We were all freezing and ready to give up and return home when we heard tumultuous cheering and applause. Tired and expectant, we rose to our feet to greet the long-delayed celebrities. We were tiptoeing to see over the people who had pushed in front of us. But instead of the presidential limousine with royal guests, a large garbage truck overloaded with refuse roared up Massachusetts Avenue. Atop the garbage stood a burly black man with white gloves waving to the crowd in the typical Rooseveltian manner, turning alternately to the right and to the left and occasionally flipping his fingers as if he were holding a long cigarette holder. He was greeted with thunderous applause—far greater than that received by the presidential entourage when it finally appeared. Roosevelt's every gesture was familiar to the man in the street.

President Roosevelt frequently visited the naval hospital in Bethesda, Maryland, for physical checkups, often early on a Saturday. After a short stay in the District of Columbia, my family had moved to the suburbs in Chevy

Chase, which was then considered out in the country. One Saturday I was amazed to hear police sirens. I discovered the president's party was passing by. It was my first close look at FDR. He was smiling as the car passed our street, and I waved. Much to my surprise Roosevelt waved back. This scene was repeated on many Saturdays, and the president habitually waved back as he passed. It became a Saturday morning ritual for me to wait for him on the curb, and I began to think of the president as my special friend.

This thought was reinforced a few months later when the president's secretary, Margaret LeHand, arranged to have several "good Democratic youngsters" in for a special tour of the White House. In those days, the standard tour of the White House included more than a quick tumble through the East Room, a shuffle through the Red and Green rooms, and a fast fox-trot onto the street. We toured the East Room, but were given a look at the Cabinet Room and then were taken to the Oval Office for a quick peek at the president. When we passed the door, Roosevelt was behind his desk, cigarette holder, smoke rings, and all. Papers were stacked high on his desk, and he was dictating at a furious pace. I was disappointed to find the Oval Office so small. Once again the famous smile crossed FDR's face and he waved at us. Naturally, we waved back. He looked regal and we were excited at this close-up glimpse of him at work. He moved easily and seemed relaxed and congenial. This was a far different picture from that of the crumpled, crippled Roosevelt entering St. Thomas Church on Sunday mornings.

St. Thomas was an Episcopal sanctuary off Dupont Circle and the church the president attended when he was in residence at the White House. Unhappily, it had a number of steep steps at the front. Consequently, the president always entered through a side door facing an alley. This made it much easier to pull his large black limousine up to a ramp onto which the president's wheelchair was maneuvered. The president was brought to the north exit in the wheelchair where he was lifted bodily by two strong Secret Service agents. Roosevelt's upper chest was enormous, with muscles developed from exer-

cise and swimming in the White House pool. But his legs were bent and pathetic. It was a heart-rending sight to see the agents undo the screws on his legs which held him secure in a sitting position, lift him to a standing position literally by holding his body suspended in the air, and then when his legs were in a straight position, tighten the screws to a walking stance. With help he would walk down the aisle, where the procedure would be reversed to enable him to sit in the pew. Once seated he never rose until the service was terminated, despite the continual ups and downs of the Episcopal service.

Roosevelt, like most politicians, loved cartoons—and he was the perfect subject—with pince-nez glasses, jutting jaw, cigarette holder, and flowing cape which he wore in an almost Napoleonic manner. Although the cartoonists poked fun at FDR, they never ridiculed his affliction. Usually he was portrayed as any other healthy American, standing, sitting, even running and jumping. Roosevelt collected original cartoons that pleased him, and he had a very large collection of drawings by Talburt, Berryman, Tom Little, Fitzpatrick, and Herblock, all well-known contemporary practitioners.

C. K. Berryman; *Washington Star*

DON'T GIVE IT A SECOND THOUGHT, ADOLF—

One cartoonist whose work he did not collect was Bruce Russell of the *Los Angeles Times,* whose anti-New Deal cartoons frequently were critical of the president. Ironically, Bruce Russell looked very much like Roosevelt and was often mistaken for him, which amused Russell as much as it irritated the president.

Jim Berryman of the *Washington Star* for a long time was Roosevelt's favorite. His likenesses were among the nation's best, Jim having followed in the footsteps of his famous father, C. K. Berryman. The Berrymans were the only father-son team ever to win the Pulitzer Prize for cartooning. The elder Berryman's cartoons were always kindly, but Jim's works had a bite. This got him in trouble with a number of presidents who felt the sting of his pen.

The Berrymans were a Washington institution. C. K. started with the *Post,* switched to the *Star,* and was a front-page attraction for many years. He created the famous Teddy Bear back in the days of Teddy Roosevelt and was better known in the nation's capital than most politicians and diplomats. Of an old Washington family, he was courtly in manner and appearance, and was liked by everyone. He was often taken for a senator because of his flowing, curly white hair, his bow tie and cutaway coat, and his baby-pink face. From the old school, he was widely respected both for his ability and for his graciousness. His son Jim apprenticed as a sports cartoonist and worked with another *Star* cartoonist, Gib Crockett. The *Star's* art department contained an in-house art gallery. It was large and took up the better part of the newspaper's third floor. High above the drawing boards, on the walls, were original drawings by all the great cartoonists of yesteryear—Homer Davenport, Thomas Nast, Fontaine Fox, J. N. (Ding) Darling, and Rollin Kirby, to mention just a few. Mr. Berryman's office was off the main art department, with his desk-like drawing board situated by a window overlooking 12th Street.

Of course, I had seen the Berryman cartoons on the front of the *Star,* but never realized there

PICTURES TO THE EDITORS

ROOSEVELT RESEMBLANCE

Sirs:

Paul Calvert, Los Angeles *Times* photographer, was quick to sense the striking resemblance between Franklin D. Roosevelt in a picture taken 20 years ago and Bruce Russell, *Times* editorial cartoonist. Russell (*right, below*) is known throughout the country for his caricatures of the President. The cartoonist says he is anxiously awaiting 1960 to see if he will resemble the President as he appears today.

TOM LEWIS

Los Angeles, Calif.

Photo Credit: *Life* Magazine

were two Berrymans. The father-and-son signatures were as close as their intricate cross-hatch style.

Having copied the elder Berryman's work, I was determined to meet him and, if possible, obtain a Berryman cartoon to hang in my room. One Saturday, with fear and trembling, I called the *Washington Star* to ask for Mr. Berryman.

"Which one?" the operator asked.

"I don't know," I responded. "Which one is the artist?"

"They both are," the switchboard girl helpfully intoned.

"Well which one is there?" I mumbled, and she connected me.

"Cliff Berryman here," a pleasant voice replied, and I explained how much I admired his work and asked if I could stop by for a visit.

"Well, I don't usually come in on Saturday," he said, "and today I am just getting ready to go shopping. But I will be here next Saturday. Why don't you stop by then?"

So we set a time. I could hardly wait.

The following week I took the long bus ride from the suburbs into town and entered the *Star's* Romanesque building. The elevator vibrated as it ascended through the old lattice

Speech bubbles in cartoon:

G-GEE, REDS, I'M SO NERVOUS! Y'KNOW MY POOR SISTER DIED OF SHELL-SHOCK LAST YEAR!

KEEP YOUR BILL UP, BABY!...MR. ROOSEVELT SAID TH' SHOOTIN' WAR HAS STARTED...WE GOTTA MAKE TH' BEST OF IT!

YEAH! BUT WE'RE LIKE TH' U.S. MERCHANT MARINE.... UNARMED!

AYTHYA CALLISNERIA (CANVAS-BACKS.... TO YOU.....AND ME!.....) FAVORITES OF HUNTERS....AND CERTAINLY OF EPICURES...HAVE 60 DANGEROUS DAYS AHEAD OF THEM...THE GOVERNMENT HAS LIFTED THE BAN ON THESE PADDLE-FOOTED PRIZES....

DON'T SHOOT BOYS! I GOTTA CHECK UP ON TH' SPECIES AN' TH' LOCAL REGULATIONS FIRST!

THA'S FINE! —AN' THEN THEY'LL BE IN GEORGIA.... AN' MY LICENSE IS NO GOOD THERE!

IS THERE ANY PENALTY FER SHOOTIN' DECOYS?...I BLASTED 4 OF 'EM THIS MORNIN'!

Jim Berryman; With Regards to the Wood Brothers —

Jim Berryman; *Washington Star*

plex design of a duck blind. We leafed through the folio.

"I know Jim would be pleased for you to have one, so why don't you make a selection. Since he isn't here, I will autograph it to you for him." So I picked the one I liked, and Mr. Berryman proceeded to inscribe a few lines at the bottom of the cartoon.

"Well, young fellow, the cabinets are full of my cartoons," he said, "so why don't you look through them and select one while I go to work?" He directed me outside his office and opened the cabinet door where the drawings were located. Then he rolled up his sleeves and sat down at his drawing board. I am quite certain he was not prepared for what was about to take place. There must have been a twenty-year accumulation of drawings in the cabinets. The original drawings were neatly stacked row on row, and I went through each cartoon in the collection. It must have taken three hours. Every now and then Mr. Berryman would stick his head outside and inquire, "Haven't you found one yet?"

Well, I was determined not to miss anything—and be sure that the one I selected was the *very best* one of all. I put aside a dozen or

work, so typical of the antiquated rock-and-roll lifts. Somehow or other the jittery old machine made it to the proper floor. I walked through the art department and into Mr. Berryman's studio, but no one was home. This made me very uncomfortable. I puttered around awkwardly for a few minutes. Then a voice from outside the door said, "Mr. Wood, I am Cliff Berryman." As a youngster of just thirteen, I was nervous and didn't know what to say. Realizing the situation, he kindly took over the conversation.

"You know, my son Jim is also a cartoonist, and I am very proud of his work. He does the sports cartoons and is coming right along. I have a few of his drawings over here which you might be interested in seeing."

And the senior cartoonist pulled a half-dozen cartoons from the top drawer of the cabinet. The drawings were of sports scenes, one of a hunting theme involving a most com-

Newman Sudduth; *Washington Star*

TO ARTHUR WOOD JR. WITH BEST WISHES NEWMAN SUDDUTH

Newman Sudduth; *Washington Star*

so, and by the time Mr. Berryman was ready to go home I had narrowed the field to six. I finally selected one featuring Adolf Hitler and Benito Mussolini. Mussolini was dragging Ethiopia's Haile Selassie, and Japan's Hirohito had China in chains. Hitler, with a helpless Austria in tow, was being advised, "You are learning fast, Adolf." The cartoon was autographed by Mr. Berryman, who was relieved to know that a choice had finally been made. The original was dated 1940. The job of placing the cartoons back into the cabinet was a mammoth one and took the better part of an hour. I wanted to put everything back just as I had found it. This was to be the first of many such experiences. Mr. Berryman had long since gone home when the task was completed.

During the cleanup, I became acquainted with several of the staff artists in the offices nearby, including a splended draftsman by the name of Newman Sudduth. "Sud" was what is called in the trade a "bullpen" artist, one of a number of staff artists with drawing boards lined up in a row. Sudduth could do anything from maps to caricatures and was on call for almost any assignment. Every task he tackled was done with expertise and finesse. As he was not a promoter, his talents were not fully appreciated by the *Star,* and he died in relative obscurity. His drawings of movie stars and visiting celebrities, however, were among the finest I had seen. For a time, he did a series of war-hero drawings which appeared in the Rotogravure section—full-page drawings in crayon which were reproduced in sepia. One of Sud's drawings of Roosevelt was widely reproduced—perhaps more than any other portrait of the president. Few remember Sudduth's talent, but I shall never forget his brilliant drawings, many of which found their way into my budding collection.

Gib Crockett at the time was doing occasional sports cartoons and turning out clever spot drawings which were used generously throughout the *Star*. He spent considerable time on these "spots" (small drawings to illustrate an article and brighten the page). Gib was irreverent, as he is today, and was a source of fun and games for the entire art department.

Gib Crockett; *Washington Star*

Gib Crockett; *Washington Star*

The bullpen of the *Star* was a talented group, with the Berrymans at the head.

H. M. Talburt of the Scripps-Howard newspapers was one of the best of the Washington graphic artists. His caricatures of Roosevelt and Hitler were world-famous. They were different from the carefully rendered drawings the Berrymans produced, but one always recognized the persons depicted. His style, which in the early days had been influenced by Ding (J. N. Darling of the *Des Moines Register and Tribune*), had developed and matured to the point where he was widely copied by many of the up-and-coming cartoonists who worked during World War II. "Tal" stayed at the drawing board right up to the time he had to retire because of poor health.

Another top Washington cartoonist of the day was a young Baltimore artist who had worked as a copy boy for the *Baltimore Sun*. He had trained under two of the best—Pulitzer Prize winner Edmund Duffy and cartoonist-designer Richard (Moco) Yardley. John Stampone was cartoonist for the *Army Times*, a service publication which, during World War

II, was located in a barn-like office off 16th Street and Military Road in Washington, D.C. John had the fountain of youth etched in his face. He looked too young to be a prominent cartoonist. With his puckish face, brown curly hair, easy manner, and contagious chuckle, he still looked like a copy boy. I worried John to death. I followed him from office to office, from 16th Street to Georgetown to K Street to L'Enfant Plaza. Wherever the *Army Times* decided to relocate, there I was peering over John's shoulder, watching him pencil his drawings, commenting as he inked, and always asking for an original. To this day, I don't know why or how John took this punishment, but he has been a good friend over the years, and the originals in my collection trace his progress step by step through a number of administrations.

Gib Crockett; *Washington Star*

3

Like Father — Like Son

MY FATHER was a great hobbyist and Sunday painter. He collected coins, stamps, and first-day covers, and also dabbled in magic. He was greatly interested in drawing and frequently would give me a helping hand whenever my school reports needed illustrations. A medieval castle he drew for my fifth grade paper was as professional as one rendered by Howard Pyle. I still have the original, which I prize highly. Sunday was his only day off, and I recall his sitting by the hour at a desk in the living room decorating stamp album pages with carefully rendered designs. Everything he did, he did with perfection, and those pages were as beautiful as the designs of the stamps themselves. He should have been an illuminator, as he had both patience and ability. Too bad he made his living as an attorney!

At any rate, while he decorated the pages of his stamp albums, I would sprawl on the floor making drawings of whatever caught my fancy in the magazines or newspapers. Frequently I copied the comic pages, which were colorful, and in those days, expansive. A comic feature would have a full page all its own. One of the tragedies of "progress" has been the radical reduction in the size of newspaper drawings.

Copying is often discouraged by art teachers, but it was a boon to me, and I later discovered that imitation was a common practice with most budding artists. I sat by the hour drawing my favorite comic characters in action while Dad pored over his stamps.

It was a first-day cover and a book about Robert E. Lee that propelled me further into the hobby of collecting original drawings. My father was organizing a stamp exhibition for display in the old Post Office Building on Pennsylvania Avenue, a few blocks from the White House. One of the items to be exhibited was a first-day cover of the Byrd expedition to the South Pole autographed by Adm. Richard Byrd, brother of the long-time senator from Virginia, Harry Byrd. Fred O. Seibel, the distinguished Virginia cartoonist, had drawn a cartoon on the Byrd expedition for the *Richmond Times-Dispatch* which had been reproduced in one of the Washington papers. Dad had seen the cartoon and thought it would enhance the post office show and decided to try to obtain the original for the opening of the exhibit. He was also anxious to have a newly purchased book autographed by the editor-author who was located in Richmond. The book was the first volume of the life of Robert E. Lee by Douglas Southall Freeman. Dr. Freeman, an eminent historian, author, and Pulitzer Prize-winner, was a fraternity brother of my Dad's, and they had frequently visited

Fred O. Seibel; courtesy *Richmond Times-Dispatch/Richmond News Leader*

together at Phi Gamma Delta functions. At the time he was editor of the *Richmond News Leader.*

One weekend my father decided to drive to Richmond to kill two birds with one stone. He called Dr. Freeman to make sure he would be in his office, and we headed south by automobile. All the way to Richmond I was regaled with stories of Dr. Freeman. He was, indeed, an amazing personality, and the more I heard, the more anxious I was to meet him. From my father's description he was not only knowledgeable and distinguished, but also served as sort of unofficial host for any celebrities who happened to visit Virginia's capital city.

In addition to editing the *Richmond News Leader,* Dr. Freeman taught at the War College in Washington with such students as Dwight Eisenhower and Omar Bradley. He also taught at Columbia University, had two daily radio shows and, in his spare time, wrote articles and books. He was much in demand as a speaker, and lectured at major universities and forensic forums from coast to coast. He was considered by many the first citizen of Richmond, and I was awed when we were ushered into his office.

For many years the *News Leader* and the *Times-Dispatch,* the two capital dailies, had operated from separate buildings, but shortly before our visit the two papers, for economic reasons, had put their heads together with quarters in the same building. Dr. Freeman's office was large and spacious, with an Oriental rug you sank into rather than walked upon. The good doctor greeted us warmly, giving both of us the fraternity grip—which was a surprise to me, as I was unaware of either the handshake or its meaning. He was gracious and fatherly, standing tall but slightly bent, and with a high-pitched, scratchy voice. He was almost bald and his head glistened in the sunlight, which lit up the room from the window overlooking Fourth Street. His desk was oversized, and the office resembled a living room or the lobby of a country club. I was greatly impressed with the entire scene.

Dr. Freeman and my father had many mutual friends. For a few minutes there was an interchange of greetings and small talk. Then Dad handed the noted editor the book he was anxious to have autographed. I had heard how Dr. Freeman rationed every minute in order to achieve a maximum workday, and we did not want to take too much of his valuable time.

Dr. Freeman took the book and went over to his swivel chair behind the desk. Then a most unexpected event took place. The distinguished scholar, historian, and editor, the epitome of the Southern gentleman, leaned back in his chair. He leaned back once, he leaned back twice, and he leaned back the third time, and then spit all the way across the room. His aim was true, and the path was straight as an arrow. A loud "twang" rang out like a firebell as he hit the brass spitoon some fifteen feet from the front of his desk. I have never been so surprised in all my life. I was not even aware as he spoke that he was chewing tobacco, but that loud metallic ring brought the fact into sharp focus. It took every ounce of restraint to keep from laughing out loud, and I didn't dare look at my father for fear of hysterics.

Dr. Freeman, completely unaware of the shock his actions had produced, proceeded unperturbedly to autograph the flyleaf of the book. He wrote in a Spencerian hand, so small that it was difficult to see—much less read—the inscription. I didn't even try. I did notice, as he handed me the book for the ink to dry, that his teeth were stained from the tobacco. My father thanked him for his kindness and asked if he would be willing to contact cartoonist Seibel in order to have the Byrd cartoon autographed.

"Why certainly," the editor said as he reached for the phone. "Fred is somewhat of a recluse, and I don't know whether he will see you. But let's try." The phone conversation was somewhat muffled as Freeman lowered his voice while speaking on the telephone. He put down the receiver and said, "You're in luck. Fred is in and has agreed to see you. He doesn't have an office here at the paper," Freeman laughed, "as he doesn't want to have too much to do with us. He stays to himself most of the time and we only see him coming and going.

You will find him in a penthouse studio on top of Richmond's only skyscraper."

We thanked Dr. Freeman and walked the three or four blocks to Richmond's tallest building. It was a slow elevator to the top floor. A small, gnome-like gentleman peered cautiously around the door as if we were intruders, but welcomed us when we identified ourselves. Mr. Seibel's office was moderate in size, with a spectacular view of Richmond. File cabinets lined one wall, and his cartoon originals were stacked neatly in tall columns near his drawing board. The board was ink-stained but neat. The entire office gave a feeling of orderliness.

Seibel was slight, with sandy hair, and he squinted over an enormous pointed nose. He was short but had huge biceps and muscles—like a "90-pound weakling" with the arms of Atlas. His glasses were perched at the end of his nose, which made him appear bird-like, and his blue eyes darted back and forth nervously as he looked us over. He looked much like the crow he used as an identification symbol in each of his cartoons.

My father was a remarkable man. He had a warm, easy manner that quickly put everyone at ease. He possessed an infectious laugh which he used frequently, and it always broke down any barriers or tension. Although Seibel was reputed to be a difficult man to deal with, it was only minutes before Dad and the hawk-nosed cartoonist were acting like life-long friends.

Mr. Seibel was sure he still had the Byrd cartoon, and he shuffled through the large accumulation of drawings he had neatly stacked in groups of fifty or sixty. He used a heavy-ply illustration board, and it required an effort to lift a large number at a time. Seibel signed his cartoons "Fred O. Seibel" and his handwriting was as distinguished as his carefully lettered signature. Finally locating the Byrd drawing, he took it over to the drawing board. He erased the penciled caption and cleaned the drawing with an art gum eraser, removing the "crumbs" with a dust mop formed of turkey feathers. After relettering the caption in India ink, he affixed his signature with the same message he used for signing each cartoon, whether to the president of the United States or to an engraver in the composing room who requested a cartoon: "To Mr. J. A. Wood, with my compliments, Fred O. Seibel."

Little did I realize at the time that one day I would work at the side of this talented little man and see him affix that same autograph to hundreds of cartoons requested by fans all over the country.

4

A Profitable Hobby

To BECOME a cartoonist, it helps to have a proclivity for drawing and sketching. For me, copying other artists—particularly the comic artists—became almost an obsession. Almost every waking moment after lessons were completed—or, frequently, when they were not—was devoted to drawing and studying the local newspapers.

With a "hunt and peck" technique and an old office Royal typewriter to play with, my first newspaper saw the light of day in the fifth grade at Phoebe Hearst Elementary School. Luckily, the co-editor was South Trimble Lynn III, whose father was a noted Washingtonian and whose grandfather was the Capitol architect. We would carefully prepare the copy, and the six-page newspaper was taken to the Capitol and printed on a mimeograph machine. It was, to us, a handsome product, profusely illustrated. We solicited advertisements from every commercial house within miles of the school. The ads cost from ten cents to a half-dollar—a sizeable sum in those days. The school encouraged the project, and the copies, hot from Capitol Hill with the latest sports news, gossip, and cartoons, were eagerly checked by fellow students to see if they were mentioned in the dispatches.

Newspaper publishing was fun, and profitable as well. My family's move from the District of Columbia to suburban Chevy Chase made it necessary to recruit a new editor in the new locale.

As luck would have it, a prospect was quickly forthcoming. Sitting next to me in the Rosemary Elementary School classroom was a shy, red-headed kid with freckles and a contagious laugh. He was always drawing, and I was impressed with his facility and skill. His drawings were in pencil, and beautiful, far superior to anything of mine. He was interested in my effort to launch a paper, and we held several planning sessions after school. We became fast friends, which was most fortunate, as he was responsible for the spread of the cartoon bug and my resultant collecting virus. My new friend was named Peter Clapper, and his father was the well-known and widely respected columnist for the Scripps-Howard newspapers, Raymond Clapper. Pete lived not far from the Chevy Chase Club, and we worked on the paper either at his house or at mine, which was close to the school.

The newspaper required a tremendous amount of work, but it was a beneficial experience. The highlight of each issue, at least to us, was a cartoon feature we both worked on called *It's a Fact*. It was a direct steal from Robert L. Ripley's *Believe It or Not*. In our version, unusual facts were gleaned from the encyclopedia and profusely illustrated. Pete

Fred Packer; New York Mirror

did the portraits and the "scenery," and I was responsible for the decorative cartoons scattered throughout the text. In short, he did most of the work, and I handled the doodles and lettering.

Pete shared my enthusiasm for journalism and drawing. Thumb-tacked to the walls of his room were a number of original cartoons by the nation's top cartoonists drawn especially for him. Today Peter Clapper is a well-known radio commentator.

Most of the artists represented in his collection were affiliated with United Feature Syndicate, a subsidiary of the Scripps-Howard newspaper chain. Ray Clapper contacted United Feature Pres. George Carlin, and I was invited to visit the New York syndicate offices with my father. If Pete could get cartoons for his room, I wanted to be second in line.

Carlin, long-time head of the syndicate, was a chubby, red-faced gentleman full of enthusiasm and bubbling over with a desire to talk about the syndicate business. He personally took us on a tour, explaining how a syndicate worked, progressing from the art department to the mechanical aspects of the business— the mats and columns mailed to papers throughout the world. It was a fascinating day.

At that time, most of the comic artists had offices at the large newspaper syndicates. A visitor who managed to gain access to the art department could meet an entire hall-full of cartoonists, for the stalls stretched as far as the eye could see. Famous artists worked side by side. At United Feature, for instance, were Paul Berdanier, the political cartoonist, and Alan Maver, a sports cartoonist. In the comic field were Jack Sparling, who with Drew Pearson did a strip called *Hap Hopper, Washington Correspondent,* Moe Leff, who drew *Joe Jinks,* and H. M. Brinkerhoff, who produced *Little Mary Mix-up.* Also in the lineup was Ernie Bushmiller, an attractive, curly-haired cartoonist who drew *Nancy* and *Fritzy Ritz.*

Each of these artists graciously contributed a drawing to the growing Wood collection. Carlin not only helped with his staff of cartoonists but also put me in touch with

Mollie Slott, mother hen of the *Chicago Tribune*'s New York News Syndicate, which was located in the same building. He later was to introduce me to King Features Syndicate executive Bradley Kelly and Sylvan Byck, comic editor of the Hearst Syndicate, located three blocks away on 45th Street.

Mollie Slott of the *Daily News* was one of three top lady executives in the syndicate field in the 1940s. The other two were Mildred M. Bellah of the McNaught Syndicate and Kathleen Caesar of the Bell Syndicate. Mrs. Slott was diminutive in size but a powerhouse in personality and ability. The bespectacled comic editor was for many years the right-hand to the *News'* legendary Colonel Patterson, who was responsible for producing many of the top comic strips of that period.

Mrs. Slott had a good feel for successful features and knew most of the comic artists in the business. The News syndicate was very tight with its original comic artwork, but Mollie had her artists do special sketches of their comic characters for me, many of them in color. I am sure they were less than delighted with this extra assignment since artists are traditionally behind schedule with mountains of work. The usual practice was to mail specially printed

Chester Gould; reprinted by permission: Tribune Media Services

cartoons to readers who wrote fan letters. An assistant would letter the reader's name into a "hole" left for a salutory greeting, and most were happy with the reprint. But an original drawing is far different from a copy. The drawing itself sparkles and possesses a lifelike quality that no reproduction can emulate. In addition, the original is precisely the way it comes off the drawing board and, consequently, there is a spark of genius, an intricate part of the artist's personality wrapped up in the finished product.

To me, there could be no substitute for the *original,* and Mollie Slott shared this feeling. A battery of New York News artists complied with her request for a special drawing to decorate the walls of my home studio. Mollie was one of the best comic editors and was a tremendous help to me over the years. She had a son about my age, and she always treated me as one of her boys. Like George Carlin, she enlisted the aid of many syndicate artists, and I was able to obtain a fine group of drawings from her large and able stable of artists. They included Milton Caniff, who produced *Terry and the Pirates,* and such artists as Bill Holman (*Smokey Stover*), Frank King (*Gasoline Alley*), Chester Gould (*Dick Tracy*), Al Posen, Stanley Link, and a number of equally important artisans.

I was delighted when United's George Carlin introduced me to King Features Comic Editor Sylvan Byck, another top newspaper executive. Byck was short and tough and looked like Edward G. Robinson's twin brother. He was a chain smoker, and when he took a deep drag on his cigarette he was most ominous. I am sure he scared off many a prospective cartoonist with his fierce look. This, however, was a facade. Actually he was warm-hearted and a devoted cartoon enthusiast. In fact, he had at one time been a political cartoonist for the *Seattle Times* and in his spare time a serious and expert watercolorist. When he retired, Byck was one of the most respected men in the field.

Like the other syndicate executives, he took us to another floor where the artists were located and introduced us to Leo McManus, production manager and head of the department. McManus looked very much like pictures I had seen of his famous brother George,

creator of *Bringing Up Father*—"Maggie and Jiggs." McManus gave us a rundown on the various artists in the stable, and we met Fred Packer, the Pulitzer Prize-winning cartoonist, and Clyde Lewis, who shared his office and drew a feature called *Buck Private.* Going from cubby hole to cubby hole, we also were introduced to Paul Frehm, who worked with Ripley on *Believe It or Not,* and Bob Dunn, who worked with Jimmy Hatlo on *They'll Do It Every Time.* I also met Joe Musial, who assisted with a number of features, including *Popeye,* as well as Dave Breger, famous for *Private Breger,* and McGowan Miller, who did a panel called *Noah Numbskull.* All were star artists with King Features. The King Features crew contributed more drawings to the collection, and I was fast approaching the number of cartoons displayed in my pal Pete Clapper's bedroom.

I continued to work on school publications, and I learned more and more about the production side of newspapering. I was also working harder and longer on my cartoons. The newspapers were mimeographed, and any drawings used had to be cut through a thin wax sheet with a stylus—not much progress, I thought, since early Egyptian days. If you have ever tackled a stencil with a stylus, you know how difficult it is to render a "masterpiece" that compares favorably to the drawing you are trying to do. My junior high school had only one stylus and my reproduction efforts were feeble. First, a drawing was made in pencil, then inked so it would show through the cloudy wax paper. This drawing was then inserted beneath the wax paper and traced. It was hard to see, even with an improvised lightboard, and more often than not the hours of drawing were lost in the faulty reproduction. Frustration was the name of the game, particularly if you wanted to show samples of your work, and what budding artist doesn't?

This was vividly brought to mind when I learned that a collection of original cartoons was to be displayed at the Wythe Gallery in downtown Washington. The artist with the one-man show was one of my favorites, Arthur Szyk, a displaced Pole who had come to

America to escape the German war machine. His biting anti-Nazi war cartoons were magnificent in technique, an intricate overlay of line and color much like Bible illumination. His work appeared as covers for *Colliers* and in the newspapers *PM* and the *New York Post*. I had admired his drawings, which were widely reprinted and distributed during World War II. The British Ambulance Corps was sponsoring the art display to raise money for Polish war relief.

The first day of the exhibit I was at the gallery as the door opened, anxiously awaiting the work of this artist whom I idolized. His originals far exceeded my expectations. The caricatures were brutal; the drawings of Goering and Himmler were as hard-hitting as any of Goya's *Los Caprichos*. His paintings were unbelievably beautiful, layer upon layer of color so structured that they resembled tapestries. I was ecstatic.

Because of the early hour, I was virtually the only one in the gallery. One rotund little man was closely examining the pictures. Drawing near, I noticed he was wearing very thick glasses. As I came to where he stood, I noticed his face was pressed right up against the drawings.

"Be careful with those originals," I warned. "You might smear one, and that would be a calamity! Don't you think Szyk is a great artist?" I asked the little man, pointing out a particular drawing with Hitler and Goering dressed as Nordic heroes. "Look at that texture and detail," I admonished, pointing to an interesting design on a decorative shield.

The stocky, bald-headed man grinned and continued to look at the drawings. After I finished my dissertation, he stuck out his hand and announced, "I am Arthur Szyk." (I often thought how fortunate it was that I liked his work.) I told him of my interest in cartooning. He asked if I had any of my drawings with me. I replied that I did not.

"Well," he said, "I'll be in town all week. Maybe you can stop down again. I would like to see what you do."

The very next day I bundled up a group of my junior high school cartoons and headed back into Washington on the bus. When I arrived at the Wythe Gallery, Szyk was autographing copies of his book *The New Order*. It was a long time before the crowd thinned out enough for me to reach him. At last I screwed up my courage, and with mimeographed masterpieces in hand, pushed my way up to the artist.

"Ah, my young friend," he said, "I see you are back." He reached out to inspect the cartoons. Spontaneously and without thinking, he muttered in his thick accent, "My Gott, zey stink!" Noticing at once that I was crestfallen, he qualified the critique, going into considerable detail to show how I could improve the figures and layout. We became close friends, and I corresponded with him for years. Later, I met his wife and family and obtained a splendid group of his original political cartoons for my collection. I still think his drawings are among the best satirical work of our time. As some measure of proof, he and Sir David Low, the British caricaturist, were singled out as targets of Hitler's wrath.

Szyk's criticisms were most helpful. I took his advice and worked harder on figures, design, and perspective.

My high school drawings were quite different from the crude mimeographed sketches I showed Arthur Szyk. The newspaper was printed letterpress, and the quality and fidelity of my artwork took a great leap forward. I did cartoons for the paper and was art editor of the school yearbook. I also experimented with color and layout. It was an opportunity to learn while working, and the experience was a boost to my spirits and drawing ability.

5

Going by the Book

HOW DOES a young person train to be a cartoonist? That question caused me great anxiety. There were no ground rules and few textbooks to shed light on the subject. I had checked at the local library and, while plenty of art books were available, none could be found with any practical advice on my favorite subject. What would be the next step?

Since the Library of Congress in downtown Washington was reputed to have *every* book published, I decided to apply for a summer job to continue my search and to earn some badly needed "pin money." The only position open for a youngster of sixteen was that of elevator boy and hatrack attendant. I took it.

It was a wise decision for it provided access to the stacks. In my off hours I ransacked the card catalog looking for books on cartooning, and I struck the mother-lode. The library had on file all the old issues of *Puck, Life,* and *Judge*—the definitive American humor magazines. I discovered the works of Zim, Opper, T. S. Sullivant, J. S. Pughe, Will Crawford, and other early masters of cartooning. I filled out the library slips and ordered bound magazines by the cart-load. The stacked books reached high above my head on the ornate desks in the main reading room.

My only art education was obtained by studying the drawings of these versatile craftsmen. I would advise any young person interested in the field to seek out these old books for reference and study. Reproduced in this volume are some of the works by these deft humorists. Note the expressions, posture, action, and character delineations.

Race was not a delicate issue in the late 1800s and early 1900s, and the caricaturists brought out the eccentricities and humorous qualities of the English, Irish, Scotch, Negroes, Jews, Swedes, and Indians. Everyone was subject to the satirical slant of their poised pens. "Crosshatch" and "Ben Day" were in vogue even in those bygone days. These techniques gave "color" to the outline of the figures. Crosshatching is a pen technique of patterned lines to give a texture. Ben Day is a mechanical dot printed on a wax paper, also to denote texture. It is added to the drawing by pressing the areas designated for shading with the screen and removing the excess with a razor.

Specially treated paper with a dot- or line-design or pattern also can be used with the application of acid to the paper in areas where the shading is desired. This is called craftint, or grafix, and comes in single or duo-shades. Even in the early days of cartooning, these shadings were in vogue.

Puck and *Judge* are marvelous sources for

study of expression, body positions, and varying techniques, as well as layout, or the arrangement of the cartoon.

The Library of Congress was also helpful in turning up other books and sources. I would recommend the following books for the serious student of the cartoon:

- *Fun With A Pencil,* by Andrew Loomis, The Viking Press, New York, 1940.

- *Figure Drawing For All It's Worth,* by Andrew Loomis, The Viking Press, New York, 1943.

- *The Zim Cartoon Course,* Cartooning, Comic Art and Caricature, Horseheads, New York, 1914.

- *How To Draw Cartoons,* by Clare Briggs, Garden City Publishing Co., Garden City, New York, 1937.

- *How To Draw Cartoons Successfully,* by Carl Anderson, The World Publishing Co., Cleveland, Ohio, 1935.

- *Advanced Animation,* by Preston Blair, Walter T. Foster, Box 456, Laguna Beach, California, 1949.

- *You Can Draw Cartoons,* by Lou Darvas, Doubleday & Company, Inc., Garden City, New York, 1960.

Other books helpful for research are:

- *Cartoon Cavalcade,* by Thomas Craven, Simon and Shuster, New York, 1943.

- *A History of American Graphic Humor,* by William Murrell (2 vols.) Whitney Museum of American Art, 1933.

- *The Human Figure in Motion,* by Eadweard Mybridge, Dover Publications, Inc., New York, 1955.

In addition to many hours of concentrated study of these books, I sought out local cartoonists for advice and counsel. Washing-

J. S. Pughe; *Puck* magazine

Will Crawford; *Puck* magazine

ton was a mecca for cartoonists and a center for the best in the trade. I pestered them all: the Berrymans, father and son, and Gib Crockett of the *Star,* H. M. Talburt of Scripps-Howard newspapers, LeBaron Coakley, Gene Elderman and Herblock of the *Post,* Yardley and Edmund Duffy at the nearby *Baltimore Sun,* and John Stampone of the *Army Times.*

Several cartoonists had advised: "Go to art school, learn to sketch rapidly, and study light and shade, perspective, and the human figure." The leading art course in town was at the Corcoran Gallery, and I enrolled for Saturday classes. The instructors were excellent, but the exercises in discipline were only that. The first day a plaster cast of Socrates was placed in the middle of the studio on a tottering wooden stand. We drew Socrates from every possible position and in every conceivable light. The second Saturday we sketched Socrates again, and then did so once more on the third Saturday. By the time the fourth Saturday rolled around I never wanted to look at the face of Socrates or any other part of his anatomy. I decided then and there to retire from formal art training.

I continued to pursue cartoonists to learn how they approached ideas and techniques, the tricks of the trade. Persistence and determination paid off. I got helpful advice, and usually an autographed original drawing as well.

Fred Packer; New York *Mirror*

UNTER DEN LINDEN

6

James Montgomery Flagg
AND THE ASSOCIATED PRESS

JAMES MONTGOMERY FLAGG

THE ASSOCIATED PRESS is located just off Rockefeller Center in New York City at 50 Rockefeller Plaza. A modern, square-shaped building matching the architecture of the Center, it has always been one of the most accessible newspaper offices in the big city. For one thing, if the person with whom you had an appointment was out to lunch, you could always watch the ice skaters in the rink below until he got back. In the spring and summer the flowers, pretty girls, and gawking tourists made standing on the corner a pleasant pastime.

My father had an acquaintance in the Rockefeller Plaza complex whom he had met in Havana. His Cuban friend, Mr. Cantevares,

ran a curio shop that sold almost everything, including shrunken Indian heads carefully preserved in small jewelry boxes stuffed with cotton. I can still recall the cold feeling on first seeing one, and the horror of hearing how they were prepared. Whenever Dad visited his friend from Havana, I would visit the Associated Press, a much more agreeable locale where the heads were still intact.

I had been told that AP housed a large variety of editors, cartoonists, and artists, and was anxious to see for myself. One of New York's better-known political cartoonists was the AP's Hank Barrow, who turned out punchy crayon cartoons for the news service. I arrived at the AP armed with a three-by-five-inch card,

David Mark; courtesy The Associated Press

SOFTENING UP THE UNDERBELLY

with Barrow's name carefully lettered at the top, and a list of two or three recent cartoons that had struck my fancy.

Not knowing my way around, I stopped by the desk of the newspaperman nearest the door. His name was David Mark. I explained my mission, and he was most sympathetic as he did cartoons himself, in addition to his writing and editorial tasks. He took me to a fellow editor who was more closely affiliated with the art department, but before I left I asked Mark for an original drawing. The spot drawing he gave me was one of the first of many obtained over the years from this talented stable of artists.

I did meet Mr. Barrow, who was about to leave for an appointment. He picked originals of the two or three cartoons that were on my list and stuck them in an envelope. He was gracious but in a hurry and turned me over to another artist, John Milt Morris, who at the

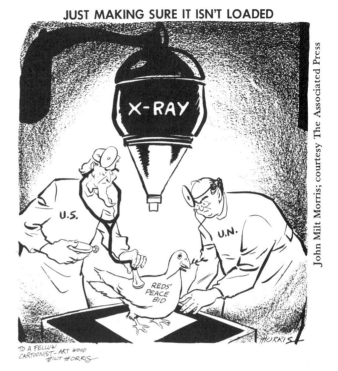

JUST MAKING SURE IT ISN'T LOADED

HIS LATEST VICTIM

time was doing a daily panel called *Neighborly Neighbors* and a Sunday page as well. In addition, he contributed numerous spots to the clip sheet distributed by the AP. Morris was a

very fast worker. His clean brush strokes alternated with intricate crosshatch designs. It was fascinating to watch him work. In order to get rid of me, he introduced me to Pap, the sports cartoonist whose desk was located nearby. In later years John Milt Morris was to become a close friend. He succeeded Hank Barrow as chief editorial cartoonist for the AP.

Pap, whose real name was Tom Paprocki, was well known, and his sports cartoons on pebbled board included intricate portraits of sports stars and action-packed little drawings of athletes crawling all over the page. His printing was letter perfect, clean, precise, and decorative. I was greatly impressed. Pap, although polite, had a brusque way, and after I had pestered him for a cartoon, he let me know in no uncertain terms that I had better head for home. I later understood why the other artists routed visitors to Pap's desk.

I returned often over the years to the AP to visit these men and to obtain artwork. They were good-natured to put up with the curious and persistent kid from Washington. The AP had a number of sidebar features—panels and comic strips—as well as political spot drawings and illustrated graphs rendered by a large staff of cartoonists and illustrators. It was quite a shop.

Many of the top comic artists of the day worked for the Associated Press, including Fred Locher, who drew *Homer Hoopee*, R. B. Fuller, who drew *Oaky Doaks*, Frank Robbins, who drew *Scorchy Smith*, Charles Rabb, who drew *Adventures of Patsy*, and Don Flowers, who drew *Modest Maidens*.

I was particularly impressed with the work of R. B. Fuller. His drawings, while whimsical in nature, were beautifully drawn in the general style of Charles Dana Gibson and Montgomery Flagg. Fuller in earlier years had turned out wash drawings for *Life* magazine and *Judge* and was also a fine pen-and-ink

OAKY DOAKS

R. B. Fuller; courtesy The Associated Press

draftsman and designer. His drawings of *Oaky* are among the best in the history of the comics. His girls were beautiful, his monsters masterful, his castles solid and decorative, and his dialogue, while not sophisticated, was funny enough to carry the story. His artwork was rich and humorous, and I think he has been much neglected.

The originals by the AP's noted artists were stacked nearby in a small stockroom which was referred to as "the back room." The editors made the mistake of taking me into this repository, inviting me to take my pick of any of the drawings that I liked. It was like Brer Rabbit in the briar patch. On one occasion I took several weeks of artwork that had not been processed and had to mail back the originals. What a glorious time I had sorting through the stacks of drawings to select the best ones for my collection. No wonder I returned so often to the AP.

Soon I learned that editors are glad to see you for a brief period but discourage a lengthy intrusion. I began to stop by just long enough to pay my respects and then make a hasty exit. It was on one of the perfunctory visits that I spotted one of my favorite artists sitting alone in the office of the editor. His eyebrows were mop-like, his eyes flashed, and his abundant gray hair was brushed back in ringlets. He held his cigarette at the edge of his lips with ashes flicking down his face. It could only be James Montgomery Flagg, who had used himself as the model for the famous "I Want You" recruiting poster of World War I. I was certain that it was he, and I walked in, stuck out my hand, and said, "You must be James Montgomery Flagg." He was startled, and he took what remained of his cigarette out of his mouth. "I recognize you from your poster," I said, "and couldn't let an opportunity like this pass. I have always wanted one of your original drawings and wonder if you would give me one."

"You are a brassy kid," he laughed, "but I admire your guts. I sell my work, you know," he chuckled, "but if you are that interested how about having breakfast with me tomorrow morning at my home studio and we will discuss it then."

His response took me by surprise. I had been told by friends that Flagg was impossible, egocentric, acid-tongued, and hostile. I was warned that it would be impossible to get to see him, much less get a drawing. But my friends were misinformed. No one could have been more gracious, more interested, or more helpful than James Montgomery Flagg. I told him I would have to check with my father, who was in New York with me.

"Bring him along," Flagg instructed me. "I will expect you at 9:30. My address is the Parc Vendome, 340 W. 57th Street."

And so it was that I met one of my favorite artists, a man who remained a close friend until his death, hastened by dissipation, wenching, and serious eye problems. Flagg was one of the most famous New York characters. I loved his honesty, his warm, winning way, and his great sense of humor.

Early the next morning I was up at the crack of dawn pacing the room. We were staying at a small hotel, the Wellington, on Broadway. There was a little Chinese restaurant, "The Three Decker," located around the corner which served a delicious fresh fruitcup and the most reasonable breakfast in New York. Afraid that perhaps Flagg didn't mean breakfast after all, my father and I fortified ourselves at the fresh fruit emporium.

As it turned out, Flagg really meant breakfast. We walked over to the Parc Vendome, his residence a few blocks from Central Park, and he was waiting for us dressed in a red robe and a wrapover neck scarf. He looked most distinguished with his flowing gray hair and bushy brows—the picture of an artist's artist. His hands were wrinkled and boney, and his knuckles and veins stood out when he motioned us into the living room. Flagg's apartment, with very high ceilings and wall-to-wall paintings, was overwhelming. Even more impressive were the two nude models posing in the living room.

"Take a break girls," he instructed them, as he ushered us into the dining room. As it was the first time I had seen a nude, much less two generously endowed lovelies, I paid little attention to the breakfast fare. These beautiful girls were lounging in large stuffed chairs that ringed his studio. One was smoking a cigarette, with her leg over the arm of the chair, and the other was reading a magazine, a scene right out of a Renoir painting with similar color in similar places. It was hard to concentrate even on James Montgomery Flagg.

Flagg worked at a large easel situated in the center of the main living room. Although he was primarily known for his pen-and-inks, he was working in oils and, much to my surprise, he was using a palate knife. Most of the illustrators at the time used a brush. I noticed every detail, including the palate, which was covered with a rainbow of color, and the rag, with which he wiped the paint, draped over the canvas. The ceiling was almost two stories high. The north light streamed into the room through the large front windows. Flagg's paintings were everywhere—portraits of wives and girl friends were lined up one, two, three, side by side. All were of attractive women. The portrait Flagg called attention to, however, was one of his father placed prominently to the right of the ladies.

"That's my dad," Flagg announced, pointing to a man with strong features not unlike his own chiseled face. "A hell of a man. One of the best. He's over ninety and swears he will beat a hundred. With his luck, the old bastard's probably right. We are from a hardy stock, mean as hell, but we live forever," he laughed, patting his chest. "And I am meaner than he is. So I guess I will be around for a while too. I certainly hope so because I have a lot to do. Now, kid, what do you want to see?"

Before I could answer, he pulled a folder from the back of a table and took out a file containing a group of photographs.

"You might be interested in this," he said, "with a Southern accent like yours." He took out a picture of a portrait of Robert E. Lee. I knew it was a splendid likeness, for my father had indoctrinated me into the Lee legend, having attended Washington and Lee University in Lexington, Virginia.

"Let me tell you about this," he growled, eyes flashing. "I painted this for the Virginia Museum in Richmond because I always admired Lee. He was a gentleman and a hell of a general. I did this from a daguerreotype, which was extremely tough because it was so small. As you know, light reflects, and it made it difficult to study his features. I spent a lot of time on it, and I offered to give it to the museum free. But a son-of-a-bitch in Richmond wouldn't let them accept my painting," he fumed. "And do you know why? Because the buttons on the uniform were on the wrong side! Did you ever hear of Douglas Southall Freeman?"

We admitted that the name was familiar, but Dad didn't comment further since Flagg was so agitated.

"Well that bald-headed baboon rejected my painting because of those damn buttons. You see, the photographer who did the daguerreotype printed it in reverse, and so the uniform was buttoned up the wrong way. I should have noticed, but I was so engaged with the face that I didn't catch it. Well, Freeman was one of those picky men who couldn't overlook details. He was on the board of the museum, and they turned down my painting of Lee because the buttons were on the wrong side! So I sold it. That will fix them," he bellowed.

Ironically, the painting later became the property of Washington and Lee University, where it still is part of a permanent collection. It is in pretty good company with the Pine portrait of Lee and Rembrandt Peales' famous portrait of Washington dressed in the red uniform of a British colonel.

Flagg had worked himself into such a rage that he paced back and forth like a tiger. He had a terrible temper when aroused, and this was one of those times. He lit another cigarette and pulled out another picture from the file. "Here's a picture of the old man with one of my favorite models, Gilbert Bundy's wife. You know Bundy's work, don't you?" (At the time I was not really familiar with Bundy, but I later acquainted myself with his work and got to know the talented young artist who took his own life, perhaps as a result of Flagg's infatuation with his wife.)

JAMES MONTGOMERY FLAGG

I asked Flagg for a picture of himself at the drawing board, and he autographed a photograph with his familiar signature.

"How I wish I had a short name like Art Wood," Flagg said. "I have spent half my life signing my name. I don't know why when I started I didn't just use plain Jim Flagg. That's what you get for being a showoff," he said.

I reminded Flagg of his promise to give me a drawing.

"Did I say that?" he asked with a pained expression. "I never give a drawing away, and why should I give one to a tousle-headed kid like you?"

"Because you said you would," I responded, "and I know you are a man of your word."

He laughed out loud with an almost explosive force. Then he said something that has become almost a collector's motto for me; I have never forgotten his words. "Son," he said, "if you don't ask, you will never get. Many of my artist friends have been scared to ask me for a drawing. But you asked, and you are going to get one of my best."

He pulled out a large portfolio and leafed through a parcel of drawings. He didn't let me see any of them at first, but selected a very large pen-and-ink which he removed from the package.

"This is one of my favorites. I think it's one of my favorites because I like the female model, and I think the male figure is well-modeled. So if you like it, it's yours!"

I was so excited I could hardly hold the original, which was almost as big as I was. I put it down on the table and turned to Flagg.

"It's beautiful," I said, "and I am thrilled and proud to have it." And I was! "Now please autograph it for me."

"Autograph it for you? My God! See, my signature is right at the bottom. Don't tell me you want me to write it all over again!"

"That's exactly what I want," I replied.

So he took a pen and inscribed the large original drawing, affixing that famous signature once more in the corner. Then, he impatiently brushed his sleeve aside, smearing the inscription.

"See, I told you I shouldn't have autographed it. It serves you right," he said with mock irritation. But I was happy with the personal inscription.

"Now what else can I do for you?" Flagg asked, which my dad interpreted as a signal to go. It was not my interpretation.

"Mr. Flagg," I said, "you are perhaps the best-known artist in America, and I am sure you know everyone in the business. There are a few illustrators I would like to meet, and I wonder if you might call some of them for me." (Today I cringe to think of my audacity, but at the time it seemed quite natural.) The funny part is that he did call some of the most noted artists for me on the phone: Charles Dana Gibson, Howard Chandler Christy, Dean Cornwell, Arthur William Brown, John Gannam, and Frank Godwin.

"Now listen, Art," he lectured, "you can't expect all these men to give you a drawing, but if you just want to say hello, I'll try to help you."

The first one he called was Gibson, but he was in Europe. Then he called Christy, who was out of the city, but I talked to Mrs. Christy. Then he called Dean Cornwell, one of my all-time favorites, since he specialized in religious paintings, which appealed to me. Luckily, Cornwell was in. Flagg made an appointment for me.

"Dean's a quiet fellow," Flagg advised, "and one hell of an artist—not like that damn photographer Norman Rockwell. But you won't get a drawing out of him, so don't ask. I have been after him for ten years to get an original for my studio, and he has never come through. So forget it. But you will enjoy meeting him and seeing his studio. I bet he spends more dollars transporting his canvasses than he gets in commissions," Flagg laughed.

So I took the address provided by my friend, and Dad and I moved from one studio to another. When we left Dean Cornwell's penthouse, I had one of his original drawings under my arm. I never told Montgomery Flagg.

7

The One, the Only, the Original

WHAT IS there about an original drawing that makes it so special? As this chapter title indicates, it is "the *one* and *only*." No original drawing is like any other. Each has its own individual charm, quality, and style. There is a vitality and life to an original piece of art that cannot be duplicated, no matter how faithful the reproduction. In addition, there is the thrill of being close to the master's hand—a short step away from the creator. Good drawings possess a zest and beauty that is indescribable. Words do not suffice to capture the feeling or spirit, for the drawings have to be seen to be appreciated—and it is an intimate personal experience.

In short, I was "hooked" as a collector. I not only enjoyed meeting noted cartoonists and illustrators and obtaining their originals, but many, like Arthur Szyk, were helpful in criticizing my work and making beneficial career suggestions.

At first, it required great effort to screw up my courage, knock on the door of a complete stranger, introduce myself, and attempt to converse while working up to a request for advice and a sample of the artist's work. It was a touchy undertaking, but worth every bead of perspiration.

Initially my collection consisted of just a few scattered drawings which were either framed or attached in acetate to the slanting wall of my bedroom. But with the help of prominent syndicate executives and frequent trips to New York and other cities to visit the artists personally, the collection began to take shape. I was anxious to obtain a representative sampling of each artist's work, and in almost every case I succeeded.

Some of the artists were crusty. Noted illustrator Arthur William Brown growled, "I hate collectors! They accumulate drawings like squirrels hide nuts, or like postage-stamp collectors with their stamps glued down in grimy notebooks. They don't value anything given away, and I don't give my stuff away—I sell it!"

He did, however, give me an original drawing of his famous *Saturday Evening Post* character, Mr. Tut, even if he later, in an agitated state, threw me bodily out of his studio. Years later, when I again ran into him after becoming an established professional, he was horrified to learn that I was that same brash youngster. To rectify this untoward incident, he gave me a number of his own wash drawings and some pen-and-inks by his old friend James Montgomery Flagg.

At times, it was necessary to use ruses to gain entrance to a prominent artist's quarters, which were usually off limits to strangers. The *New York Daily News* always had police stationed in the corridors of the newspaper. I would often take my coat off, wrap it up, put it

under my arm, carry a large brown envelope and walk right past the cops, pretending that I was the messenger boy. Many of the illustrators lived at a palatial address on West 67th Street which had guards everywhere. One ruse I used at the apartment was this:

Guard: "What do you want?"

"I've got a message for Howard Chandler Christy. He's expecting this package!"

Guard: "He's in 2A."

I would go right on up. Another stratagem I used as a youngster was to call up an editor and say in a very deep voice, "This is Arthur Wood of Washington, D.C., and I would like to see you about an important matter. I wonder if you would be free at ten?" Most saw me because they thought I was with the Internal Revenue Service.

If distance made it impractical to contact artists personally to obtain drawings, the mails were used as a vehicle. My letters were in longhand and posted to a home address if at all possible. A personalized sketch in color or pen-and-ink was included to call attention to my note, as many popular artists received thousands of requests each week. If a cartoonist used a special character or symbol, this would be utilized with a hand-lettered "balloon" asking for an original.

Sometimes ten to twenty letters over a period of several years were necessary to gain a response, and frequently the answer was a polite "no." More often than not, however, the artist complied, and I was successful in my endeavor.

I hounded any artist who visited the nation's capital. If the papers mentioned that a particular favorite was in town, I would telephone all the hotels until I discovered where he or she was in residence. Then I would call and make an appointment. If that didn't work, I'd just show up in the lobby of the hotel in hopes of catching the artist in transit. Most were gracious and cooperative—even making special drawings for me. Ham Fisher, creator of *Joe Palooka,* visited Washington, D.C., during the war, and while at the Willard Hotel did a sketch of Joe Palooka in military uniform, especially autographed for me. Previously, he had answered one of my missives with a long letter admonishing me to enclose postage, noting his mailing bill for such requests was so expensive it would have paid for two or three college educations. From that time on, I was careful to enclose enough stamps or cash to cover mailing costs. If the postage cost more than my initial contribution, I then mailed the difference. This helped enormously and doubled the number of my replies.

Most of the artists were happy to send a drawing as it was good publicity and assured a steady reader and advocate.

The mails were not always kind to original drawings. Many arrived crushed or torn, and others were bent double. Most could be flattened with pressure so that the creases would vanish, but a few times the drawings were not salvageable. There was a George McManus daily comic strip that I had long awaited. It finally arrived from the West Coast, but was mangled in its roll. In an effort to straighten it with a hot iron, I scorched the paper, giving it an ugly amber tint. A *Colliers* cover in color that had been painted on masonite and mailed to me was cracked in half. Another beautiful wash portrait of Richard Burton was ripped to shreds. Numerous political cartoons were torn or damaged in the mails. I learned to make every effort to pick up originals in person to avoid the wear and tear.

While the mails were unkind to the drawings, my postmen were unusually cooperative and helpful in assuring that once they had their hands on the package, it would be delivered with care. They would not cram oversized parcels through the slot in the door, and many times they went out of their way to make sure the drawings were not dampened in rainy weather. One mailman in particular, a wonderful black postman named Fields, who

Hamilton "Ham" Fisher;
Joe Palooka—reprinted with special permission of the McNaught Syndicate

became a fast family friend, took a special interest. I would meet him a block away and give him a full military escort to the front door. He took as much pleasure at my delight in receiving an unexpected package as I did and even cautioned his co-workers at the Chevy Chase post office to take special care of Art Wood's "cumbersome cartons," as he called them. Over the years, he delivered hundreds of drawings—from postcard-size to mattress-box-size—and he often waited to see if a package contained a *Popeye* or a *Prince Valiant.* He has my undying gratitude.

In selecting drawings, I've always leaned toward the dramatic. The appearance of the drawing itself often was the determining factor, with the idea playing a secondary yet important role. This was a decided help when it came time to display the originals, for such forceful drawings would catch the eye of a gallery goer, whether the fine lines of a Nell Brinkley pen or the broad strokes of a Fitzpatrick crayon. In looking over literally thousands of originals, I have been greatly influenced by the dynamics of the pictures and the emotional effects they have on the eye. Consequently, I believe the drawings in my collection are among the better work of those artists represented.

In illustration, the preliminary sketch or preparatory drawings for the "finish" often have more life and vitality than the completed work. Most artists tend to tighten up when they do a final rendering. Consequently, some of the best drawings in the collection are in the rough-sketch category rather than the completed illustration, although both types are represented in considerable number. This is also true to a lesser degree with the comic and political cartoon, since the way the cartoonist thinks is revealed in his layout drawing, and these are fascinating to the art student as well as to the layman.

The backs of the original drawings are frequently as revealing as the finished products on the front. Often a preliminary sketch is roughed in but the artist may change his mind about design or layout and start over on the reverse side of the drawing board. The first sketch, however, reveals the artist's original concept. Frequently the cartoonist makes notes on the back that also reveal his thinking. During World War II, when there was a paper shortage, many artists used both sides of the paper. Comic artists also reduced the size of their originals for the same reason.

Sadly, the common practice in the past has been for the individual artists or their pub-lishers to destroy the original drawings after a period of time. Storing the artwork has been a problem for newspapers and for the spouses of cartoonists who see the drawings stack up in the closet or cupboard. The end result has been that much of the most valuable original artwork has been thrown out or incinerated. Syndicates that accumulated the drawings often destroyed them after publication to make room for new material.

Observing this process, I persuaded a number of syndicate executives to select a group of representative drawings for my collection each time the cupboard was to be cleared. Many times I was on hand to go through the stack myself to select the most desirable pieces.

During the war, the navy also was pushed for space. Regular housecleanings were the "order of the day." Vast accumulations of newspapers, magazines, and drawings were piled into the large wastebaskets headed for the incinerator. I burrowed through these large bins, salvaging cartoons, illustrations, and spot drawings (small drawings illustrating an article). I placed them neatly in piles in the hall after work. Then I wrapped them in brown paper which I brought from home where I was billeted. I saved large numbers of original drawings from being burned by rummaging through the "garbage" in this fashion. It was dirty work but paid handsome dividends. Some of the finest drawings in my collection otherwise would have been thoughtlessly destroyed. After the war, I received a call from the U.S. Office of Archives saying that the government would like to have the material back. My response was a polite but firm "no!"

8

"All the Cartoonists Fit to Print"

NEW YORK summers are unlike any others in the world. The streets are furnaces and the buildings retain the heat. Add to this the high humidity and the subway soot and you have an unholy combination that causes an out-of-towner to wonder why he ever left home. But when business beckons, the businessman succumbs. During the summer of 1942 my father traveled to that long, thin, pulsating thermometer stretching off the New Jersey coast, and I went with him.

The cartoonist whom I wanted to meet more than any other was the *New York Times* editorial cartoonist, Edwin Marcus. He drew only one cartoon a week. It appeared in the "News of the Week in Review" section of the Sunday *Times*. His prestige and decorative political depictions had always attracted me to the good gray *Times*. He had a unique style of up-and-down background strokes that distinguished his work from all the other contemporary artists. His Uncle Sam drawings were world famous; his was the only cartoon on the editorial page, and no cartoonist was reprinted opposite him.

The rest of the news section featured work by the world's noted cartoonists, interspersed with related articles on world events. Such luminaries as Sir David Low, Leslie Illingsworth, Strube, Fitzpatrick, Rollin Kirby, and Oscar Cesare were regular contributors to the

Times. Their best work was reprinted in the news section, but Marcus' work was given the key spot on the editorial page.

Ed Marcus already had achieved considerable fame from his theatrical drawings, which for twenty-five years had been prominently placed in the theater section. He had an interesting way of working. The persons to be

PORTRAIT OF ERICH VON STROHEIM

Ed Marcus; reprinted with permission of the Marcus family

49

depicted were invited by the *Times* to appear in person for a sitting, and Ed Marcus worked from life. The glamorous stars of stage and screen would come to a special studio at the newspaper where they would pose for the artist who made on-the-spot sketches and also photographed the celebrities for reference. As a consequence, he was close to the great and near-great and counted as personal friends most of the political and theatrical notables of his day. And his day was the longest in the history of the business—fifty years with *one* newspaper—perhaps the most famous newspaper in the world.

Marcus also worked at home in Riverdale, New York. His ideas were submitted to editor

THE GOAL

Ed Marcus; reprinted with permission of the Marcus family

"AREN'T YOU GLAD YOU HAVEN'T ONE
OF THOSE THIRD-TERM PROBLEMS?"

Lester Markel each Wednesday, and the finished cartoon was delivered on Friday for the following Sunday. Usually on Wednesday Marcus had lunch at Sardi's right across from the entrance to the office of the *Times*.

My father called Marcus at the *Times* during a heat wave in the city. Dad came out of the phone booth drenched from the brief conversation, which required the phone booth door to be shut to keep out the surface noise. "Marcus will meet us at the *Times,"* he said, wiping his brow. We then caught a cab to the big daily's 45th Street entrance. Marcus was in the library of the paper and he greeted us warmly on arrival. He was a short, peppery, immaculately dressed little man, who seemed to bounce with enthusiasm as he walked. He had a very sharp nose, pince-nez glasses, and his hair, black and patched with gray, was smoothed back Italian-style. In fact, Marcus was of German extraction. He apprenticed with Winsor McCay, McCauley, and Outcault—the big three of early cartoondom. During World War I, Marcus' political cartoons ran an entire page, the first, and to my knowledge the only, political cartoonist whose work was ever given full-page display.

Marcus liked young people, and he was anxious to encourage my enthusiasm for

Edwin Marcus at work.

"IT'S YOUR TURN"

cartoons. He took me back to the file where his drawings were stored and selected several cartoons he especially liked. One was a cartoon of Uncle Sam with a bullet through his hat fired by the "Isms." The caption read, "Remember that gun was given you to help protect me." It was a typical Marcus Uncle Sam, with the trademark up-and-down pen strokes in the background. The original was surprisingly small and delicately rendered and was stamped with the date and the *Times* insignia on the back. This encounter was the beginning of a long and rewarding friendship.

Ed Marcus; reprinted with permission of the Marcus family

Marcus had a most complete morgue of photographs at his home. In it were pictures of every celebrity and almost any subject you could describe—animals, war machines, costumes, uniforms, and the human figure in every conceivable posture and pose. It was a library that would have been a credit to the *Times'* own file of clips and pictures.

Marcus' cartoon likenesses were exact and a holdover from his portrait days. His method was to make a detailed drawing of the face at a size convenient for a good likeness and then pantograph the drawing to the desired size of the cartoon. He had a special German glass which projected the face to the spot above the body in perfect proportion. He was an expert in using this "flexi" (as he called it) to render the carefully constructed facial expressions onto the paper. Marcus usually worked at his idea in grease pencil on rough copy paper with labels so that the editor could immediately grasp the idea. Then, after approval, he would transfer the idea to tracing paper at the desired size of the standard cartoon. This was "carboned" onto the illustration paper, usually of Strathmore stock. When wash technique was required, he would use watercolor paper with a fine texture. But pen-and-ink was his specialty, and he was a master. He worked fast, once the basic concept was derived, and often used his wife, Edna, for feminine poses.

Marcus' ideas were difficult to conceive because they had to hold up over the weekend. Drawn on Wednesday, they still had to be timely and pertinent on the following Sunday. Usually he was on top of the news and seldom was required to do a "filler."

When Marcus retired in 1958, the cartoonists of the nation presented him with two albums of specially designed cartoons commemorating his fifty years with the *Times*. His signature was engraved in gold on the leather cover and the tributes in every style were drawn on the stationery of the nation's cartoonists. It was an accolade justly deserved after a career of fifty years with one newspaper that carried Marcus and "all the news that is fit to print." Ed Marcus died in November of 1961.

9

Cartoons for the Navy

WHEN I finished my senior year at Bethesda-Chevy Chase High School in 1944, I faced the problem of being drafted or enlisting. I took the latter course. I was duly influenced by my best friend, Bill Metzel, whose father was an admiral on the staff of Adm. Ernest J. King, Commander-in-Chief of the U.S. Fleet and Chief of Naval Operations. Adm. Jeffrey Metzel was one of the most dedicated men I have ever met, and I was determined that if I was to go into the service, the navy was for me. Bill and I decided to sign up together with the hope of serving on the same ship. So we both enlisted in the navy, were sworn in at the same time, and had high hopes of duty in the same battle area. Our hopes were dashed, however, when I came down with pneumonia and was hospitalized at Bethesda Naval Hospital. Bill went on to Bainbridge, Maryland, and the East Coast Naval Training Station, and I was left behind to fight the aches and pains. It was over a month before I arrived in Havre de Grace, the loading station near the navy base at Bainbridge.

The discipline of navy training was tough, and the group with which I was associated was one of the toughest. I was working out with the Seabees who were older than I—most of them in their late twenties or early thirties.

Whenever the "smoking lamp" was lit or there was a spare minute, they gave me sage advice about my love life. The advice was as tough and raunchy as the men themselves. At the time I was dating my high school sweetheart and I could never live up to the

SALTSHAKER

Art Wood; courtesy U.S. Navy

55

Art Wood; courtesy U.S. Navy

expectations of this unruly gang of over-sexed roughnecks. I must say that all the advice and counsel dished out during this neophyte period stood me in great stead when I lectured at Bainbridge's Separations Center many months later on the topic "How to Adjust to Civilian Life." I was an authority at eighteen!

The training at Bainbridge was geared to the war effort, and there was little time or energy for drawing. After a full day on the "grinder," running the obstacle course, there was little breath or time left to indulge in cartoon interests. I doodled in the barracks and did caricatures of the men in my company whenever there was a spare moment. This practice caught on, and I was trapped into doing a drawing of every man in my company. These caricatures were then sent home to lonely parents who ached for a word from their sons away from home. It also saved the men from writing, as most of the lazy recruits just

scribbled a message at the bottom of the cartoon. It was a great way for them to goof off and yet touch base with the folks at home.

This effort achieved a certain notoriety as even the officers wanted to pose for these pen portraits. As a result of this mass cartoon effort, I was summoned by the editor of the

SALTSHAKER

Art Wood; courtesy U.S. Navy

HELEN HIGHWATER

Nick Pouletsos; courtesy U.S. Navy

base newspaper for an interview. The newspaper was properly named the *Bainbridge Mainsheet* because it was located in the main section of the base which was off limits to skinheads (a term of endearment used to describe recruits and what was left of their golden locks). So I had to take off my boots (a hangover from World War I) in order to walk on this "holy ground," and I felt out of place when I reported to Commodore Behrens' office. He was the chief executive officer of the base.

As it turned out, I did not immediately gain access but was given the evil-eye by Sp1c.

Elizabeth Harrison, a fine artist who specialized in portraiture. We hit it off, and she requested that I contribute regularly to the base newspaper. This was a real break for me. The newspaper already had three cartoonists, all of them professionals. One was Nick Penn, whose real name was Nick Pouletsos, who had ghosted a number of noted comic strips. The other two artists were equally well known. All were waiting to "ship out," and the newspaper staff was anxious for a backup.

Nick was a super-slick cartoonist. He did a pretty-girl panel called *Helen Highwater* and a clever strip about a stupid sailor called *Stalemate*. He specialized in attractive girls, and his sexy cartoons were pasted on bulkheads throughout the world. He did everything with finesse. As a result, he was assigned to *All Hands* magazine and the SEA Syndicate in Washington, where he became staff artist. This, too, was a break for me for I ultimately took his place in Washington when he was discharged on "points."

I turned out two or three cartoons a week during basic training, and when I finished my stint, I was assigned full-time to the newspaper. Its offices were palatial compared to the barren barracks. I was in seventh heaven. Commodore Behrens liked my cartoons, and I was given a special pass to "mess" and also a special pass to go off and on the base. Few officers had it as good.

My cartoons which appeared in the *Bainbridge Mainsheet* were distributed by the Bureau of Naval Personnel and were picked up and reproduced in base newspapers around the world. As a result of this attention, I ultimately moved to Washington to work as a staff cartoonist for *All Hands* magazine, the official navy publication.

I did have an interesting interlude while waiting for overseas duty. I was assigned to a road gang constructing highways through the base area. The project was under civilian direction, and my job was no different from that of a prisoner or hardened criminal—to break up rock with a sledge hammer. The huge rocks, which had been brought in by train on a spur line, were too heavy to lift, so we were ordered

STALEMATE

to crush them into gravel. One of the men sharing the duty was a violinist who was frantic for fear that this type of work would ruin his hands, but those in charge turned a cold ear to every entreaty. So for eight hours a day, with a short break for lunch, we were red-eyed and red-handed. My hands, which had been toughened by boot training, were a mass of bloody blisters, and so were the hands of the violinist. The civilian overseer was heartless, and I wondered how a civil engineer could utilize naval personnel for this type of work. But legitimate duty or not, we were out in the blistering sun on a naval chain gang. It was the hardest work I have ever done, and I doubted if the swelling in my fingers would ever subside.

It took several weeks for the feeling to come back. The violinist was sent overseas. I often wondered what became of him or whether he was able to continue his musical career. I was eventually assigned to the Bureau of Naval Personnel in Washington, my old hometown.

10

Persecution on the Potomac

IF BAINBRIDGE was heaven, BuPers (the Bureau of Naval Personnel) was hell! I was the only non-commissioned staffer on *All Hands* magazine, the official voice of the navy. That I was low man on the totem pole is putting it mildly.

The navy bullpen was reminiscent of the old syndicate days—drawing boards end-to-end, with various illustrators and cartoonists lined up toe-to-toe, wall-to-wall. My drawing board was second to the last, which showed my "up front" rank. At the back of the row was Dave Rosenberg, a kindly anchorman who comforted the harried art staff. It was a motley crew indeed!

The editor of the magazine was a captain whom I will call Leaderman. Leaderman was crude, vulgar, and officious—a fat, schmaltzie package. No one could understand how he happened to obtain his position of prominence, but there were rumors he was related to a political warhorse in the executive suite. At any rate, like the mountain, he was there.

Leaderman had trained as a psychiatrist and was an expert on everything but people and journalism. He was insecure and ineffectual and, to protect his image, assumed a position of arrogance and superiority. Fortunately, he had inherited a competent staff of seasoned news men and women, who had served on such national publications as the *New York*

Times, Life magazine, *Time* magazine, the *Washington Post,* and *Newsweek.*

The weekly staff meetings over which Leaderman presided were out of *Alice in Wonderland.* He lectured at great length, waving the air and assuming a Napoleonic stance, complete with hand-in-shirt gestures. He was the Captain Queeg of BuPers—without the marbles.

I was the lowest in rank in a department of several hundred, and it gave him sadistic pleasure to lean on me. One day he called me into his office, a large cubicle located at the far end of the city room where the staff was lined up in chairs at the side. "Wood," he intoned, "I have a great idea for you to draw in your cartoon. You have a sailor, see, chipping paint, see, on a ship. There, you have it! Go draw it up." Even the yes-men had a puzzled look. It was no idea at all, only a situation and not a particularly original one at that. This was Leaderman's concept of a great gag cartoon.

His favorite pastime was taking one of the staff artists' original drawings and writing across the face of it in bold strokes "Not Funny" with a grease crayon. As any artist knows, a grease crayon cannot be erased, and so the drawing was for all purposes destroyed.

There were many talented men on the *All Hands* staff. One of the most versatile was Dave Burton of Salt Lake City who was a direct

Dave Burton; courtesy U.S. Navy

descendant of Joseph Smith, the Mormon leader. He could draw like crazy with a lovely line and an uncanny sense of design. Like most of us, he turned out everything from maps to missile sketches, working rapidly and with confidence. He was comfortable in any medium but was best with the brush. Dave was one of the fastest draftsmen in the service, and a workhorse to boot. He ghosted a girlie panel, *Helen Highwater,* and the comic strip *Stalemate* featuring a pint-sized sailor who was always on the make. Dave's work was clever and funny, and he was much admired by his co-workers. He was never too busy to give a helping hand, criticize a drawing, or show how it could be improved. He was a one-man art school, and I took advantage of his generosity.

The other Dave on the staff was Rosenberg, a wise counselor and constant consoler. In addition to his art talent, he was a noted dancer who in his spare time taught folk-dancing to senators and congressmen. He had enormous energy and enthusiasm and used to leap around the office with such abandon that it tired the rest of us. He was the assignments editor, but unlike most, took on many of the tougher tasks himself. He specialized in airbrush and was adept at using this medium for the navy magazine covers. When Leaderman was around, Dave's thin mustache quivered nervously, and he leaped even higher in the air.

Other staffers of national note were: Fred Keziah, who was an animator and gag writer for the *Saturday Evening Post;* Hank Ketcham, father of *Dennis the Menace;* George Sixta,

who later created the dog strip *Rivets;* Frank Owen of *Colliers;* and Dave Stern of comic-book fame.

Gene Kelly, the Hollywood dancer and producer, also was serving a hitch in the navy. He was producing animated training films and Disney-like cartoons using the then-rare and expensive multiplane camera which gave a three dimensional effect. At the time, he was working on several animated features preparatory to the invasion of Japan. These were abandoned when President Truman decided to drop the atom bomb at Hiroshima.

At *All Hands* magazine and at the Ships Editorial Association, a service syndicate, each artist was expected to be a jack of all trades. We knocked out a vast array of graphics, including gag cartoons, comic strips, magazine covers, political cartoons, maps, V.D. posters, illustrations, and various training manuals. I did a panorama of drawings, spots, and funnies, including a cartoon panel, *Saltshaker,* and a Sunday page, *All Thumbs,* a navy take-off on *Sad Sack.*

Some of us were recruited for special projects of a top secret nature. After being sworn to secrecy, we were given diagrams and charts and were briefed by scientists in order to translate in picture form the complex technical material. The drawings were done in segments, and we were carefully monitored. We were never cognizant of the magnitude of the project until the mushroom cloud over Hiroshima made the drawings obsolete. We had been illustrating the atom bomb in understandable cartoon form.

Even Leaderman with all his political influence was not invincible. The axe eventually dropped, and a cry of jubilation was heard by officers and enlisted men from Arlington on the Virginia side to Kensington on the Maryland side. Leaderman was retiring! Everyone in the office was maced into contributing to the farewell party, which was to be held in a private home off Sixteenth Street in the northwest section of Washington. No one was happier than I to celebrate. I bought cigars for everyone in the office—eight boxes—which was an extravagant expenditure on a sailor's pay. I'm sure Leaderman wondered why everyone in the office, including the Waves on staff, appeared the day after the announcement smoking cigars.

The night of his retirement party was cold and snowy. The streets were icy and slick and the trees were drooping with icicles. The home where the party was held was on an incline, which made it difficult to park. While a number of staffers boycotted the occasion, I went to see who would show up. To my surprise, Leaderman was almost cordial, a far cry from his office behavior. As the evening wore on, however, he sensed the hostility of the staff and began to drink heavily. While others were comparing sea stories, no one noticed that the captain had disappeared. Where was Leaderman? We looked all over the house, but he was nowhere to be found. To the dismay of the ladies, it was noted that the fur coats that had been neatly stacked on the beds upstairs had also disappeared.

We spotted the honored guest outside in the snow, hovering over a fire. There were no logs, only overcoats, stacked and ablaze. The captain was staggering over them with a bottle and an empty book of matches.

It was soon thereafter that I also was "retired" from the navy and entered Washington and Lee University in Virginia as a freshman.

In addition to his kind counselling and criticism of my artwork, *Washington Star* cartoonist Jim Berryman told me that President Truman was a cartoon enthusiast who carefully followed the graphic political commentary and the comics in the then-four Washington dailies. Jim had mentioned that the president possessed a fine cartoon collection and suggested, perhaps facetiously, that "Harry and I" get together to compare notes. So that Christmas (1947) I sat down and wrote President Truman a note on the back of my hand-drawn Christmas card, proposing just that—a meeting with him at the White House to see his collection. Almost immediately by return mail I heard from Matthew Connally, the president's appointments secretary, proposing that I stop by to see the president and his collection one afternoon early in January. I couldn't believe it.

At the time I owned a broken-down Plymouth which was badly in need of repair. Fortunately, my grandmother was visiting us from Lynchburg, Virginia, and I borrowed her Oldsmobile, which was much more presentable for a trip to the White House. At the appointed time and with her freshly washed Olds, I cruised down Connecticut Avenue to the executive mansion.

In 1947, security was relaxed at 1600 Pennsylvania Avenue, and one could drive right into the White House driveway for parking if clearance had been obtained. My name was on the list at the West Gate "pill box," and I was told by the guard to park right at the front entrance. So I drove in as instructed and parked. Another car followed close on my bumper and parked immediately behind me. As I got out, a courtly gentleman came up, tapped me on the shoulder, and said, "I see from your license plate that you are from Lynchburg, Virginia. Who are you going to see?"

"Well," I said, apprehensively, "I have an appointment with the president, and Mr. Connally instructed me to contact a Mr. William Simmons, the president's appointments secretary."

"Well, I am Bill Simmons," the stranger explained, extending his hand, "and I, too, am from Lynchburg. It's good to welcome a friend from the old hometown." We exchanged pleasantries about the hilly Virginia city. Mr.

Simmons said, "You have plenty of time. You are early and there is someone else from Lynchburg I want you to meet."

We walked inside, and he took my overcoat and called someone on the phone at the security officer's desk. A distinguished-looking black man appeared in the outer lobby. Mr. Simmons introduced him as a friend of many presidents who had been around the White House for a great many years. Samuel Jackson shook my hand and stood straight as an arrow. His hair was snow-white and he was immaculately dressed. We had a good visit together and during the conversation, he asked about my family. I told him my grandfather's name, and a big grin crossed his face.

"You are Frank Jennings' grandson?" he asked incredulously. "Your grandfather gave me my very first job at Barker-Jennings Department Store many years ago," he exclaimed. "And, Mr. Wood, you are going to have a guided tour of the White House you will never forget." And he was right!

He took me to the private living quarters, upstairs and downstairs, and even to the sub-basement. It was the first time I had inspected the president's home from top to bottom. What fun it was occupying the president's chair in the Cabinet Room, sitting on Lincoln's bed, hearing about the ghosts, and inspecting President Truman's clipping room where all the national periodicals were perused and relevant articles snipped out to brief the president.

Finally, I was ushered into the area immediately outside the Oval Office where President Truman had hung a number of cartoons from his collection. Included were originals by Fitzpatrick, Herblock, Dorman Smith, Fred Packer, and the Berrymans. Over the door was a golden horseshoe. The president was late, and also waiting to see him was Secretary of Defense Forrestal, who only a short while thereafter, in May of 1949, jumped to his death from a window in the Naval Medical Hospital in Bethesda. He seemed, however, in excellent spirits that day and informed me of his own cartoon collection that he valued highly.

President Truman was a history buff and prided himself on doing his homework, particularly concerning American history. Perhaps this is why he took such an avid interest in political cartoons. He was well-versed in the historical aspects of cartooning and as familiar with the old masters of the art as he was with the contemporary fraternity.

One thing that particularly impressed me about Truman was that he collected cartoons attacking his administration as well as those supporting it. Most politicians are only interested in the favorable comments, a trait going back to the dawn of civilization. Witness the early Egyptian and Sumarian records that emphasize the victories but never the defeats. But Truman liked cartoons, even if they were mean or derogatory, and he asked the cartoonists for the originals, hard-hitting or not. He often chuckled that he liked the tough ones the best. Most of the drawings on display at the White House, however, highlighted some specific legislative achievement or newsworthy event.

Because the president was so late, there was little opportunity for small talk. That had to wait until 1953 when as cartoonist for the *Pittsburgh Press* I sat and visited with him in his hotel room. On this occasion, I had brought along a cartoon showing him "Flying the Coop" after eighteen years of government service and was anxious to have the drawing autographed for my studio.

"Hey, I really like that cartoon," the president said, "Let me have the original for my collection."

"Nope," I said, ignoring protocol. "This is one I want *you* to autograph for me. I will be happy to send you a photostatic copy," I added, "and no one but you and I will know the difference."

He laughed out loud and said, "Okay, you win, but send me the cartoon and I will frame it outside my office."

I thought he was only being gracious, but I did photostat the drawing, eliminating his personal greeting, and mailed the cartoon to him. Much to my surprise it was framed and placed with the other drawings outside the Oval Office. Years later, when the nation's political cartoonists visited Independence,

Missouri, and were guests at the Truman Library, I received another surprise when I saw my cartoon hanging in the same spot (in the replica of the Oval Office) as it had in the White House. This cartoon was also featured on a CBS television memorial program the day President Truman passed away.

When he died, I drew a cartoon straight from the heart. It simply depicted two empty boxing gloves with HST's dates inscribed thereon. The caption read, "Fighter to the End." I had a lovely note from Mrs. Truman regarding the cartoon and expressing the sentiment that the president loved cartoons. I knew he did.

A FIGHTER TO THE END!

Art Wood; courtesy U.S. Telephone Association

11

The Daddy of the Comics

BUD Fisher

WASHINGTON AND LEE University in Lexington, Virginia, had been funded by a grant from George Washington. After the Civil War, Robert E. Lee became its president. Lee took his responsibilities seriously and established the small Virginia school as a national center for learning with a tradition of gentlemanliness—which it maintains to this day. Among his many accomplishments he established the first school of journalism in the country at Washington and Lee. This "first" was to bring me into close contact with another "first"—the daddy of the comics, Bud Fisher.

Bud Fisher is generally credited as being the first cartoonist to draw a daily strip in the format we know today. It was a close race, however. Many comic artists were on the scene at precisely the same time—James Swinnerton, R. F. Outcault, George McManus, Rudolph Dirks, Clare Briggs, Frederick Opper and C. W. Kahles. It could be argued that each was a parent of the comics.

The early humor magazines, *Puck* (1877), *Judge* (1881), *Life* (1883), and *St. Nicholas* had featured single-panel cartoons ornately and intricately drawn. The usual format was a single frame with one action or scene depicted. At the turn of the century, in the pre-radio and -television days, there was more time for reading and to study the crowded drawings filled with lengthy "balloons" and lettering.

Consequently, a large space was required for the idea to be adequately conveyed. As a rule, the cartoons were designed to fill a page, or often two pages, of the leading humor magazines.

Many of the *Puck* artists began to draw multi-panel cartoons, particularly H. M. Howarth and Eugene (Zim) Zimmerman. It was Fred Opper, however, who decided to separate his sequential cartoons with a thin wavering line to differentiate the varying actions. His cartoons employed this format as far back as 1885. It is said that William Randolph Hearst considered Opper the first true comic strip artist because of the way he split up his panels. The ziggly line gradually became better defined and evolved into thin parallel lines separating the drawings—the style used today in the comic pages. The ice skating cartoon by Opper was thought by Hearst to be the beginnings of the comic strip drawing.

It was R. F. Outcault of Chicago who created the first Sunday page comic in the U.S., *The Yellow Kid,* printed in color in the 1890s (giving life to the phrase "yellow journalism" because of the constant feuding of the two press lords, Pulitzer and Hearst, who vied for the best comic artists). Outcault's panoramic scenes of lower New York slums were an instant success, appealing to the

masses who understood the rough humor of the streets in big cities like Chicago and New York. The little bald-headed urchin who became the hero of the strip lived with his pet parrot and goat in the backwaters of Hogan's Alley. The hero spoke by means of dialogue lettered on his nightshirt colored a bright yellow, the first color process used by the daily press which until that time had featured black-and-white printing.

Outcault considered *The Yellow Kid* vulgar. Despite the success of the feature, he never related to the character and stopped drawing it in 1898. In 1902, he created another character—a more refined, mischievous youngster—*Buster Brown*. A talking dog replaced the goat, and a girl companion substituted for the parrot of Hogan's Alley. The two main characters, Buster (Robert) and Mary Jane, were based on Outcault's own children. At the same time that Outcault and Opper were developing their ideas, James Swinnerton was decorating the pages of the *San Francisco Examiner* with *Little Bears and Tigers,* drawings of animals cavorting across the pages of the Hearst newspaper. Clare Briggs, who later drew many successful features, also created the strip *A Piker Clerk* based on racetrack characters. The comic was discontinued by Hearst who felt it distasteful. The feature, however, was similar to the format of Bud Fisher's *A Mutt,* the predecessor of *Mutt and Jeff.* With a number of artists working in similar styles and format, the various ties of the railroad track converged into a single vanishing point.

Mutt and Jeff was one of the first syndicated cartoons in the U.S. Although Fisher was drawing the feature in San Francisco, it appeared in papers on the east coast and even was reprinted abroad.

Harry Conway (Bud) Fisher was born in San Francisco in 1884 and for a time did sports cartoons for the *San Francisco Chronicle.* An astute businessman all of his life, Fisher self-syndicated the feature, copyrighting the comic in his own name. He joined the Hearst organization in the early 1900s and switched to the Wheeler Syndicate in 1915, earning the princely sum of one thousand dollars a week plus a percentage of the income his strip derived. That was in the days before taxation.

With money and worldwide acclaim, Fisher travelled extensively and invested wisely. He moved in the best circles and was the guest of royalty and presidents. He lived in a plush apartment at 383 Park Avenue and married a countess. His cartoons were reprinted in book form and his feature translated into twenty-six languages. Everything he touched made money. He was the darling of society and the envy of his fellow comic strip artists.

Such adulation took its toll. According to his contemporaries, Fisher became aloof and inaccessible. He was high-handed with his friends, and irascible. He "farmed out" his work to various ghosts, the last of which was a mild-mannered artist named Al Smith who did most of Fisher's work. Fisher treated Smith like a servant and was demanding and harsh. He was a severe taskmaster, and his colleagues avoided him.

I first came in contact with Bud Fisher when as editor of a college bicentennial brochure I requested that he do a special drawing on the occasion of Washington and Lee University's 200th anniversary in 1949. It seemed appropriate to have various journalists pay tribute to the school on the event of its 200th birthday. Letters were mailed to leading editors, columnists, and cartoonists requesting special articles or commemorative drawings for the college publication. Fisher was one of the first to respond.

An old drinking companion of Fisher's had attended Washington and Lee, and nostalgia for his long-gone friend was the primary motivator. He placed a telephone call late one night to Dr. Francis Gaines, then president of the university, who was away on a trip. The call was forwarded to me. Fisher's irritable reputation had preceded him, and I was astounded to hear a pleasant voice at the end of the line say, "Mr. Wood, this is Bud Fisher. I appreciate your letter and will be happy to cooperate." He sounded as if he might have been drinking, but was amiable and polite, volunteering to do a cover for the magazine in full color. He also offered to pay the entire expense of the booklet. Typically, he wanted top placement and was willing to pay the freight. His official acceptance telegram to the university was seven pages long.

He invited me to come to New York to discuss the publication with him, and I agreed to arrange a trip at an early date. I was sure the university would not want to give him cover space, knowing the sensitivity of other artists contributing, but agreed to travel to New York to consider the project. I met Fisher at his Park Avenue apartment at 10 o'clock in the morning. I was cleared by the guard at the door and ushered into the apartment by his housekeeper.

Bud Fisher's penthouse apartment was a miniature museum. Each suite was styled in a different decor. Fisher had arranged to have historic rooms dismantled, rebuilding them in his own apartment. One room was English Manor style from the Shakespearean period, complete with stucco and cross beams. Another room was French Provincial. One exotic section was Oriental, packed with rare Chinese art treasures. The apartment was a one-floor United Nations.

Fisher was living in the back at the end of the long hall, propped up on pillows in a hospital bed. He had fallen and broken both hips. It was a far cry from the decorative, ornate surroundings of the rest of the apartment. He seemed glad to see me and offered me a scotch and soda from an open bottle on his side table. Papers and proof sheets of *Mutt and Jeff* filled the room. He was thin and gaunt and the bones in his arms protruded, as did his eyes. His thin mustache seemed lost in an emaciated face. His eyes were bright, however, and he was like a kid with a new toy. He seemed starved for attention, and I later discovered I had been his only visitor for almost a year. His cartoonist friends who remembered the shabby treatment of his heyday had deserted him in old age. Only faithful Al Smith, his assistant who lived in Demarest, New Jersey, darkened the door.

Fisher was an animated and interesting talker, anxious to tell of his past accomplishments. He described the early newspaper days in San Francisco and his interest in horse racing. He haunted the tracks by day and drew the comics at night. His early drawings were small in the original, easy to transport and compact. As the comic strip became more successful, he opened a studio, and his originals increased in size until they encompassed the drawing board—huge daily and Sunday comic strips. The transformation of his early dailies of 1907 to the gigantic originals of the late 1920s is interesting to the comic buff.

Fisher may have been influenced in "blowing up" his comic strip drawings by his experience on stage. He was a popular vaudeville personality and chalk-talk artist, having appeared on the same program in the Ziegfeld Follies with Will Rogers. In his stage performance, Fisher related his characters Mutt and Jeff to current events in the news—a trick he was to incorporate in his daily strip. He frequently included popular sports and political figures in his comic, including the president of the United States. Because the drawings for a theatre audience have to be seen by the people in the back row, it was necessary to enlarge his sketches to gigantic size. Consequently, his later original drawings are among the largest of any artist, past or present.

Fisher relished his position in high society and spent hours describing his successful European jaunts where he mixed with prime ministers and played polo with the Prince of Wales. His homecomings at dockside were big news events and were covered by the New York newspapers, wire services, and even Pathe News. Fisher regaled me with stories of his career and anecdotes from his long experience in the newspaper business. It was difficult to get away from him and awkward to leave. He kept saying, "Sit down, just one more story." In all of his reminiscing, there was little opportunity to discuss his drawing for the bicentennial. He wasn't particularly anxious to talk about it, but he did finally agree to do a black-and-white page in place of the color cover. He insisted on being placed on page one of the cartoon section, where the drawing finally appeared. It was a funny sketch of racetrack addicts Mutt and Jeff masquerading as Washington and Lee. The generals, who loved horses, too, would have been amused.

Bud Fisher died a lost and lonely man. A few of his old chums, notably Bob Dunn and Rube Goldberg, stopped by to pay their last respects before he died, but he was virtually ignored by his fellow cartoonists who had felt the sting of his fiery temper and arrogant mien. Only a handful attended his funeral. It was reported that the father of the comic strip left the bulk of his estate to the Red Cross and the Florence Crittenton homes.

MUTT AND JEFF

Bud Fisher; *Mutt & Jeff*—reprinted from collection of Art Wood

Alex Raymond; *Rip Kirby*—reprinted with special permission of King Features Syndicate, Inc.

12

Alex Raymond
SPACE AGE REMBRANDT

ALEX RAYMOND did not look like an astronaut. Nor did he resemble an atomic scientist. His impact on the space age, however, was as indelible as that of John Glenn or Werner von Braun.

Creator of *Flash Gordon* and *Jungle Jim,* Alex was slight of build and mustachioed, and he walked with a cartoonist's slouch from years of leaning over the drawing board. He was pudgily handsome and spoke in a quiet, clipped, precise manner. Modest but authoritative, he often referred to himself in the third person. He was a flashy dresser and a sportscar nut. As a comic artist, he was unexcelled. His drawings were crisp and filled with action. His women were sexy, and the costumes, if they could be called such, revealed all. His heroines were the Petty girls of the 'thirties and 'forties, complete with space-age telephones.

Alex had a rare ability to write as well as draw, and his fertile imagination pre-dated many developments in space technology. Rocket ships, lasers, death rays, space platforms, and jet propulsion belts were commonplace in his most famous creation, *Flash Gordon.*

Flash Gordon was not Raymond's first strip. With mystery writer Dashiell Hammett he had produced *Secret Agent X-9* for a two-year period, in 1934 and 1935, for King Features. Earlier he had ghosted *Tillie the Toiler* for Russ Westover and *Tim Tyler's Luck* for Lyman Young—all under the banner of Hearst's King Features. He also worked for Chic Young on *Blondie.* X-9 was stylish and caught the eye of the general public. Detective stories and mysteries were in vogue, made popular by motion pictures. The comics were quick to pick up this trend with such strips as X-9 and *Dick Tracy* by Chester Gould. X-9 stories of

SECRET AGENT X-9

Alex Raymond; *Secret Agent X-9*—reprinted with special permission of King Features Syndicate, Inc.

With drums throbbing, and frenzied natives chanting, the sacrificial procession, led by the high seer, winds toward the jungle.

Lil stumbles along as if in a dream. Stacey sobs, not through cowardice, but at the pitiful sight of his jungle-mad wife cavorting with the fanatical natives.

The high seer stops before the hideous idol. Turning, he points to Lil, who steps forward, unaided, head erect—

High in a tree top, Kolu carefully selects a long, black arrow and fits it to his bowstring.

To Be Continued.

10-29

derring-do were drawn with vitality and dramatic impact. The square-jawed detective was always in hot water—falling from buildings, out of airplanes, and into wells, giving the artist ample opportunity to show his skills in placing the figure in unusual and off-beat poses. His rendering of light and shadow created an eerie mood, full of suspense and foreboding. Even then Raymond knew he was good, as is evident by his huge signature on the early daily strips.

Despite the success of *X-9*, Raymond wanted to be his own man, so *Flash Gordon* was born in 1934—a golden-haired god surrounded by beautiful goddesses, monsters, and Oriental fiends caught up in the spaced-out world of the future. A topper feature, *Jungle Jim,* was soon to rival the main attraction in popularity.

Raymond was greatly influenced by the writer Jules Verne and the illustrator Franklin Booth, whose pen-and-ink drawings were so

SECRET AGENT X-9

Alex Raymond; *Secret Agent X-9*—reprinted with special permission of King Features Syndicate, Inc.

Lyman Young; *Tim Tyler's Luck*—reprinted with special permission of King Features Syndicate, Inc.

meticulously rendered that they resembled woodcuts. Much of Raymond's background for *Flash Gordon* was borrowed from Booth's intricately designed cities of tomorrow. But the space gear, weapons, and characters were strictly from Raymond's fertile imagination. His carefully drawn space ships, space platforms, and space artillery closely resembled the actual equipment which in time came into

being. Perhaps, the scientists of the 'sixties and 'seventies were comic readers in the 'thirties and 'forties, and the design was an unconscious emulation of Raymond's style.

Raymond was a tireless worker, turning out three features at the same time. Because of the need for careful detail in these realistic epics, Raymond spent long hours in research and painstaking art work. The strain of producing

Alex Raymond; *Flash Gordon*—reprinted with special permission of King Features Syndicate, Inc.

Alex Raymond; *Rip Kirby*—reprinted with special permission of King Features Syndicate, Inc.

X-9, *Flash* and *Jim* was too much, even for Raymond, and so *X-9* was dropped, and Charles Flanders took over the art work on *Secret Agent* for King Features. Alex Raymond continued the full-page drawing of *Flash Gordon* and *Jungle Jim,* spending the entire week both day and night on his beautifully constructed drawings.

Raymond's villains were classic. His chief antagonist in *Flash Gordon,* the Emperor Ming, was a thinly disguised Fu Manchu, an evil monarch who obliterated any and everyone in his path. Somehow, the heroine Dale and Flash always managed to slip through Ming's long and sharply honed talons. The strip was peopled with imaginative creatures: icemen (reconstructed cavemen from the ancient past), lion people, dwarfs, and a vast menagerie of robots, freaks, and monsters. The stories were fast-moving and exciting. The beauty of the artwork heightened the dramatic effect and, running full-page in color, his carefully planned panels took on the dimensions of the old masters. I clipped each Sunday page religiously from the newspapers and filed them carefully in order, never dreaming that these same pages one day would be collectors' items in book form. I had a full run of Raymond's Sunday pages and almost divorced my wife after she threw them out when we moved from Richmond to Pittsburgh.

Alex was a careful penciller—laying out his pages with architectural care and an eye to design and white space. He used a brush almost exclusively, varying the sharp edges with a dry-brush style. His characters were always in motion, leaping out of the frame with swords drawn and capes flying. Ronald Coleman and Errol Flynn would have been right at home portraying his characters.

Although the movies serialized *Flash Gordon,* Buster Crabbe with all his ability never seemed to capture the dynamic nature of the character. The serials, however, became classics and are still shown today on television and at film festivals.

During World War II Raymond joined the marines and discontinued his comic drawings in 1944. He was commissioned a captain and saw action in the South Pacific where he served as a combat artist. After the war his battle paintings were hung in the Pentagon and in the National Gallery of Art in Washington.

Returning to civilian life in 1946, Alex created a sophisticated detective strip with a social set of characters. His strip *Rip Kirby* was

RIP KIRBY

Alex Raymond; *Rip Kirby*—reprinted with special permission of King Features Syndicate, Inc.

beautifully drawn and was quickly accepted by the public as another topnotch Raymond creation. He was awarded the Billy DeBeck award in 1949 and was president of the National Cartoonists Society in 1950 when President Eisenhower entertained a group of cartoonists at a breakfast in Washington.

Alex was married to a tall, stately brunette, Helen, who had a regal manner and natural beauty that was reflected in their daughters Lynne and Judith. The Raymonds lived in Stamford, Connecticut, and although Alex worked for a time in a studio downtown, he spent a greater portion of his time at home, utilizing a studio in a spacious room with fireplace and mementos. Alex loved to draw, but not to letter. Although he did an adequate job of lettering on *X-9* and the early *Flash Gordon* pages, he preferred to have his old friend and assistant "Uncle" Larry Crosby do this tedious work.

Alex Raymond; *Flash Gordon*—reprinted with special permission of King Features Syndicate, Inc.

I got to know the Raymond family during my college days at Washington and Lee in 1948. With an eye to meeting one of my favorite artists, I twisted the arm of a faculty friend to invite Alex to the campus as a journalism seminar speaker. Alex's brother Jack had attended the university, and he was happy to accept the invitation. Raymond had never visited the historic old Virginia school, and he drove down from Connecticut with his family. I fell in love with all of them, particularly Lynne, the oldest daughter, who was about my age.

Alex was a hit at Washington and Lee. He was an erudite lecturer, supplementing his talks with quick sketches to illustrate points. He described his work technique and explained the fine points of producing a successful comic strip.

Alex was anxious to tour the historic Blue Ridge area, but I quickly discovered he was a terrible driver. He collected expensive cars and had a number of specially built automobiles tailored to his liking, but he was no match for the horseshoe curves of western Virginia. We screeched around the narrow mountain roads and were jostled from side to side in the automobile as he swerved to keep within the lines. It was tough on the passengers, and I was sitting in Lynne's lap most of the time, a situation which I wished could have been reversed. Alex's fast driving and lack of expertise ultimately may have been his undoing. Eight years later he was killed on a winding road in Connecticut when the sports car he was driving went out of control on a wet night and crashed into a tree. His driving companion, Stan Drake, noted illustrator and artist of the comic strips *Juliet Jones* and *Blondie*, was seriously injured, almost losing an ear

ON A HIGH VANTAGE POINT, FLASH GRIPS THE OUTLAW CHIEFTAIN'S SHOULDER: *"IT'S WORKING! THERE ARE ONLY TWO CARS LEFT TO GUARD THE KING'S! THROW YOUR MAIN FORCE AGAINST HIM NOW!"* GUNDAR GRINS, AS HE RAISES HIS SONOBEAM HORN TO HIS LIPS: *"BY MY BEARD, FLASH, YOU'RE A BORN MILITARY MAN!"*

FROM ALL DIRECTIONS, GUNDAR'S HORDES CONVERGE ON BRAZOR'S FORCES, SHOWERING GRENADES AND RAY-FIRE ON THE LUMBERING, METALITE MONSTERS. IN THE NARROW MOUNTAIN DEFILE, THE KING IS AT A DISADVANTAGE--

4-18-43.

WITH HIS TWO PROTECTING ARMORED CARS BLASTED OUT OF ACTION AND HIS OWN ARMOR BECOMING UNCOMFORTABLY HOT, BRAZOR WHIRLS HIS CAR ABOUT AND MAKES A DASH FOR FREEDOM!

"HE'S BROKEN OUT OF THE TRAP!" SHOUTS FLASH, *"I'VE GOT TO STOP HIM!"* *"DON'T BE A FOOL!"* ROARS GUNDAR, *"YOU CAN'T DO IT BY YOURSELF!"*

NEXT WEEK: **MAN AGAINST MONSTER ~**

Alex Raymond; *Flash Gordon*—reprinted with special permission of King Features Syndicate, Inc.

from shattered glass. Raymond was only forty-four years old. So ended a distinguished but relatively short career.

A vast fandom has grown up about Raymond, almost mystical in devotion and adulation. Other admiring cartoonists follow closely in his stylistic footsteps, and youngsters collect his pages as the ultimate in comic art. This has been fanned by the charismatic nature of the space program and the consequent interest in space exploration and technology.

Alex sponsored my early membership in the National Cartoonists Society and was a staunch friend until he died. During my senior year in college, he took samples of my gag cartoons and proposed to his editor, Sylvan Byck, that I be given an opportunity to do a humor panel for King Features. It was given serious consideration, but a job never materialized. I will, however, never forget his kindness. My panel idea was accepted by another syndicate, but in the interim I decided to go into political cartooning. I discovered that being funny all the time was not a funny business.

Alex Raymond; *Rip Kirby*—reprinted with special permission of King Features Syndicate, Inc.

13

Advice and Counsel

WHEN I first met Herblock (Herbert L. Block of Chicago), he was not the star that he is now in editorial cartooning—a talented artist, writer, hard-hitting critic, and enduring observer of the political scene.

In the early days of his career, during the late 1920s, Herblock trained with Vaughn Shoemaker, veteran cartoonist of the *Chicago Daily News* and a two-time Pulitzer Prize winner. Herb's style was influenced by "Shoes," and his work reflected the same skillful draftsmanship and design. But ideas are the main ingredient of a successful political cartoon, and Herb has superb ideas, funny when needed, biting when called for, and always dramatic and punchy. After an apprenticeship at the *Daily News*, he switched his drawing board to Cleveland and the Newspaper Enterprise Association. The NEA was a Scripps-Howard syndicate with a large list of member newspapers, and it was there Herblock won his first of three Pulitzer Prizes in 1936.

During World War II, Herblock entered the army. He was assigned to work in service publications, and his cartoons were used in training manuals and various other military publications.

In pre-war Washington, the nation's capital boasted four newspapers: the *Evening Star,* an old and respected paper; the *Washington Post,* the new boy on the block; the *Daily News,* a Scripps-Howard tabloid; and the *Times-Herald,* the plaything of publisher Cissie Patterson.

The *Post* had struggled during the war years to keep afloat, and publisher Eugene Meyer was reputed to have spent millions to keep the paper from going under. Over the years, the *Washington Post* had a number of cartoonists, some mediocre, some outstanding, and a few in the genius class: James North, Clifford Berryman, Felix Mahoney, K. L. Russell, and John Stampone. In the 1940s the *Post* had a very talented young artist by the name of Gene Elderman. His humorous cartoons on the "packed" Supreme Court, Charles Evans Hughes, and FDR were widely reprinted in the major media, text books, and encyclopedias.

Elderman had a broad, sweeping, crayon-style much like Harold Talburt of the Scripps-Howard newspapers and William Summers of the *Buffalo News.*

The pressures of producing a daily editorial cartoon proved to be too much for the tall, red-headed artist. Like many of his contemporaries, he took to drink in order to meet the deadlines and to compete with the skilled team of *Star* cartoonists: the Berrymans, father and son, and Gib Crockett. Gradually Elderman began missing deadlines and skipping town for

Gene Elderman; courtesy *Washington Post*

THE SPHINX

extended periods. The *Post* had to reprint or omit his drawings, and after much soul-searching he was fired.

The next *Post* cartoonist was a silver-haired Washington artist named Lebaron Coakley. He had at one time worked as a sports cartoonist for the Richmond newspapers. He, too, was a talented artist with the crayon. But "Coak" and Eugene Meyer didn't see eye to eye, and it was not long before the *Post* was looking for a new man.

With the war over, Eugene Meyer wanted a

cartoonist with a national reputation and staying power. Herblock, just out of the service, was his man. It was a shrewd move on the part of the wily publisher.

A keen observer of the political scene, Herblock quickly spotted the stuffed shirts and phonies. He called things as they were in tough, rough, heartless fashion. He galloped against the Washington windmills, brandishing a pen dipped in venom and a brush splashed with blood. His creations were a far cry from the gentlemanly, cavalier cartoons of the *Star*'s big three—a style that had been in vogue in the nation's capital since the turn of the century. It was some time before he deeply dented the pro-Berryman bias, but official Washington was taking careful note of this feisty Chicago cartoonist.

I called Herblock in 1950 because I admired and closely followed his work at NEA. He had been one of my special favorites since the early 'forties, and I was anxious to seek his advice about a career. I, too, had been separated from the service and, with a college education under my belt, was looking for my first job as a political cartoonist.

I contacted him at the *Post*, and he suggested we get together for lunch. The *Post* was then located in the same area as the old Willard Hotel, where Abraham Lincoln had addressed crowds from a top-story balcony. It was also near the Occidental Restaurant, which euphemistically was called "the dining place of presidents." We didn't go to "the dining place of presidents," but rather to a small counter-restaurant nearby where we could visit and so Herb could get back to the drawing board within a reasonable time.

He looked over my navy cartoons and suggested I work up a week or two of political cartoons to show prospective editors. During college I had done primarily gag cartoons in pen-and-wash for the *Washington Star*. Herb suggested I work on a pebbled board and kindly gave me samples of the glarco drawing sheet he was then using. He suggested that rather than draw in a simple line style, it would be wise to try to do some crayon cartoons for variation. He also recommended that I get in

the habit of developing four to six ideas daily for mental training, drawing the best two in fairly finished form. He even gave me the dimensions that he used in his political cartoons. With this advice, and reinforced with soup and sandwich, I headed home.

Armed with a meager photographic clip file and a week's stack of the *Post* and the *Star*, *Time* magazine, and *U.S. News and World Report*, I did a cram course in world affairs.

"Don't copy anyone," Herblock had advised, "but, if it helps, use others' cartoons to study composition and design."

This I did, and Herblock was my model. Herb's cartoons often featured dramatic cloud effects, and the rendering was letter-perfect. I practiced clouds on a sheet of paper, but mine looked hard and lumpy. They were cumulus potatoes.

I switched to animals. I did a cat-and-mouse cartoon. I never liked cats and it showed. The mouse was a Walt Disney "steal," but I couldn't find a photo of a cat in a leaping position. My rendition was stiff and an anatomical wonder. When I took the stack of finished cartoons to Herb to select the better ones, he tactfully suggested that the cat cartoon be routed to the circular file.

He picked six of the better cartoons and advised me to get the *Editor and Publisher Yearbook* and scout the papers without staff cartoonists. I went back to the Library of Congress and spent an entire afternoon combing the fine type in the *E and P* annual.

I discovered the *Houston Chronicle* had parted ways with long-time staffer Ferman Martin and that this leading Texas daily was without a cartoonist. I also found that, closer to home, the *Richmond News Leader* and the *Baltimore American* and *Evening Sun* were without cartoonists.

My dad had worked with Jesse Jones, the publisher of the *Houston Chronicle*, when he headed the Reconstruction Finance Corporation during the war years. He was also a good friend of Bill Costello, Jones' right hand public relations man and alter ego. I asked Dad to call Costello to see if the paper might be interested. He did, and it was. An appointment with

C. K. Berryman; *Washington Star*

the editor of the *Houston Chronicle* was arranged, and I planned to drive down at a future date. The only problem was transportation. I had no car.

Right after the war, automobiles were in short supply. My family thought it would be easier to buy a car in Richmond, Virginia, where a cousin was in the automobile business. A trip to Richmond was hastily planned. Since Dad knew Dr. Freeman of the *Richmond News Leader,* I thought I would stop by to say hello and "happen" to have some cartoons with me.

While in college I had been initiated into the national journalism fraternity, Sigma Delta Chi, with the young and brilliant writer Jack Kilpatrick, who also happened to be on the staff of the *Richmond News Leader,* working with Dr. Freeman.

We had had a few beers together at the initiation, and I had corresponded with him. He encouraged me to believe that there might be a spot on the *News Leader,* which had never had a political cartoonist. He suggested a meeting with David Tennant Bryan, the publisher. The get-together was arranged and I displayed the cartoons Herb had selected. All the threads came together and instead of heading for Houston, I decided to stay closer to home. I bought the car and the *News Leader* bought my cartoons. I was to remain in Richmond for six years working with "Kilpo," who succeeded Dr. Freeman as editor of the *News Leader.* During this time I married Sallie Van Dyck of New York and Petersburg, Virginia, and two of our children, Betsy and Arthur, were born in Richmond.

14

Fred "O" and Moses Crow

ᖴᖇᕮᗪ O. ᔕᕮIᗷᕮし.,

THE FIRST cartoonist I had met as a youngster was Fred O. Seibel, political cartoonist of the *Richmond Times-Dispatch*. Little did I realize at the time that I would work side by side with this talented artist. Our offices were near each other on the same floor, despite the fact that we worked for different newspapers. Competition was keen between the two journals, even though they were housed under one roof and operated under the same management.

It has been my fortune or misfortune to work for newspapers whose opposition cartoonists happened to be institutions in their respective cities. In Washington, when my work was appearing in the *Star,* the Berrymans, father and son, were both Pulitzer Prize winners, and Gib Crockett was equally well known. In Richmond, Fred Seibel was a required part of the journalistic diet, and readers turned to his cartoon before scanning the front page. In Pittsburgh, where I would later become a cartoonist for the *Press,* Cy Hungerford was better known than the president of the United States, and considerably more popular than many of the chief executives he covered during his sixty-five years of drawing cartoons for the steel city's various newspapers, particularly the *Post-Gazette.* His cartoons appeared on the front page of the newspaper for many years.

Fred Seibel had for years used as his personal symbol—almost as familiar as his signature—a sharp-nosed, bespeckled crow, which appeared in almost every cartoon. The black crow became a kind of mascot, an integral part of the daily cartoon.

Richmond Times-Dispatch

PUBLISHED MORNING AND SUNDAY

RICHMOND, VIRGINIA

CARTOONS

by

ᖴᖇᕮᗪ O. ᔕᕮIᗷᕮし.,

1952

Fred O. Seibel; courtesy *Richmond Times-Dispatch/Richmond News Leader*

THE SEIBEL TRADEMARK

In the early days of political cartooning, it was traditional for the artist to use an identifying symbol—usually an animal—which guaranteed a sympathetic readership and gave a degree of continuity. For some reason, animals have always had a universal appeal—catching the reader's eye, and the cartoonists wisely took advantage of this idiosyncrasy. The creator, in effect, produced a cartoon within a cartoon to give vent to his personal viewpoint over and above the general idea of the cartoon itself.

C. K. BERRYMAN'S TRADEMARK

C. K. Berryman; *Washington Star*

C. K. Berryman used the Teddy bear. Billy DeBeck, Ole May, and Charles Payne featured a raccoon. C. F. Naughton and C. H. Wellington utilized puppy dogs. R. W. Satterfield included a bear, Reynolds a tiger, and Plaschke a pixie with a long tail. J. S. Clubb always penned a playing card under his signature. Perhaps the most famous creation of all was Fred Seibel's crow.

In its early conception, the bird was tall and gangly, with a stork-like beak and Ichabod Crane legs. Seibel called him Jimmy Crow. Fred O. Seibel said that as a kid he had found a baby crow that had fallen out of its nest. He took it home, nursed it to health, and it became a pet. So in 1916, when he started his cartoon career, his pet was introduced to the paper's readers. When the real bird broke a leg and had to be put to sleep, Seibel buried him in his backyard, but continued to draw the crow in his daily cartoon. The crow must have been related to the talking mynah bird because he would occasionally comment on the news, reflecting Seibel's own views. The bird became so popular with readers that more attention was being paid to it than to the central cartoon. So, suddenly, the wise old bird lost his voice and never spoke another word after 1936. Occasionally, he would look perplexed or frightened, and beads of perspiration would flow from his feathers, but "Quoth the Raven, 'Nevermore.'" When a separate but equal "Jim Crow" law became controversial in the 'fifties, the popular cartoon bird also lost his name. It was quietly changed from Jimmy to Moses.

There were times, however, when Seibel thought it inappropriate to include the crow in his pictorial comment. If the cartoon was an obituary drawing or a particularly dramatic

The little black bird that appears in my cartoons is a caricature of a crow. This is my trade mark. Outside of that it does not represent anything and has no significance.

For the sake of variety, I change the attitude and expression of the crow from day to day, in order to make it fit the idea of each cartoon, which makes him appear like a sort of interested spectator or innocent bystander who watches the passing show from day to day but doesn't quite know what it is all about

FRED O. SEIBEL.

Fred O. Seibel letter; courtesy Richmond Times-Dispatch/Richmond News Leader

THE DINGBATS IN CONVENTION

Fred O. Seibel; courtesy *Richmond Times-Dispatch/Richmond News Leader*

HIS FIFTH BIRTHDAY

rendition, he excluded his feathered friend. This always brought a stack of letters from readers wondering whether Moses had died. Moses, however, did not pass away, but changed in appearance over the years like his creator. From the tall, lanky bird in the early 1900s, the crow shrank in size, becoming stocky, short, and stubby. Perhaps it was easier for Seibel to draw that way, and maybe it required less India ink.

As I indicated earlier, Seibel looked much like his feathered creation. Short and stocky, he had a sharp nose that resembled Moses' beak. His glasses were perched precariously thereon, and he peered through them owlishly. He was painfully shy and would go out of his way to avoid staffers or visitors to the paper. He would arrive very early at the office before anyone appeared, scan the out-of-town papers in the city room, and then make a few notes, occasionally clip an article, and retreat to his office on the fourth floor. He would lock the door, and no one was admitted until he had completed his cartoon. He did not believe in having lunch, as he could not relax until his drawing was complete. He usually finished about four-thirty and would slip out the back way to his favorite restaurant where he would have his only real meal of the day. Occasionally he would cheat during the workday and munch on Hershey bars that were white with age. They were carefully filed in a box near his drawing board.

While most cartoonists' offices resemble pigpens with paper—with drawings and books piled high and unopened mail stacked in heaps—Seibel's office resembled an IBM showroom. Everything was in order and in place. Only his drawing board, which was pocked with ink, indicated that an artist worked there. Even his board was covered with paper to hide the unsightly blots. One wall of the room was lined with sixteen file cabinets which contained photographs and clippings for reference, and his original drawings were stacked neatly in chronological order in tall piles on a library table. Near his board were numerous pens, brushes, and a duster formed of turkey feathers to remove

Fred O. Seibel; courtesy *Richmond Times-Dispatch/Richmond News Leader*

OUR PRESIDENT

Fred O. Seibel; courtesy *Richmond Times-Dispatch/Richmond News Leader*

ECLIPSE

erasure dust. Few people ever saw the interior of Fred O. Seibel's office. It was off limits, and everyone from the publisher to the copyboy knew it and stayed clear.

When I arrived on the scene, however, I didn't know any better. The first week, when I had problems with a drawing, I walked down the hall and knocked on his door. After all, I was new and needed help. No one answered the door. I knew he was there, because I had

Fred O. Seibel; courtesy *Richmond Times-Dispatch*/*Richmond News Leader*

THE TUG OF WARS

seen him unlock the door and slam it behind him. So I kept knocking louder and louder. Still no answer. Finally I roared out in a loud voice that echoed down the hall, "Mr. Seibel, this is Art Wood, the *News Leader* cartoonist, and I have a problem. Please open the door!"

A thin crack appeared in the door and his long pointed nose was all that showed through the opening. "What's your trouble?" he asked hesitatingly.

"Well, if you let me in, I'll show you," I responded.

Reluctantly, he admitted me with a gruff, "I'm very busy and I'm having trouble myself. I haven't got an idea, so please make it quick."

And I did. He was, however, kind and helpful, and as time passed, the door was opened wider and more frequently. We became fast friends. And he was the main reason my cartoon work took a marked turn for the better.

Seibel grew up in the small town of Oneida in upper New York. He practiced drawing the farm animals of the area, particularly the mules that pulled the tug boats up the Erie Canal. He was expert in rendering animals. He received formal training at the Art Students League in New York City. When an art job did not materialize, he worked as a machinist, photographer, clerk in a law office, laborer in a steel plant, and shoe salesman. All of these jobs, while unrelated, served to give him a broad education in observing life and the various professions. He continued to draw and finally landed a job on the *Albany Knicker-bocker Press,* where his cartoons were widely reprinted for a period of ten years. This led to his job on the Richmond newspaper, which he joined in 1926—one year before I was born.

One of the finest pen-and-ink practitioners in the business, he had a simple country-boy touch that often tugged at the heart strings. Small in stature, quiet and unobtrusive, he was a giant among graphic artists. A permanent collection of his work rests with the papers of Jefferson, Lee, and Washington at the Alderman Library of the University of Virginia—the alma mater of another talented genius, Edgar Allan Poe, who also made a black bird famous.

SEIBEL SELF-PORTRAIT

Fred O. Seibel; courtesy *Richmond Times-Dispatch/Richmond News Leader*

15

When Knighthood Was in Flower

Harold R Foster

THE CREATOR of the heroic comic strip *Prince Valiant* was tall, gentlemanly, white-haired, and soft-spoken. Somehow one expects the originator of such a strip to be a muscle-bound warrior with shield and singing sword. Appearances can be deceiving, however. Beneath Harold Foster's gentlé exterior lurked the heart of an adventurer.

Hal Foster, as he signed his work, in his younger years was an athlete and sportsman. He had been a Canadian guide, back-woodsman, hunter, trapper, fisherman, gold miner, and lumberjack. He bicycled across the country and spent weeks alone in the wilderness, subsisting on the land. Foster was a rugged individualist and an expert on almost any subject. He studied nature firsthand, and his keen sense of observation was reflected in his intricate artwork.

Harold R. Foster, while categorized as a cartoonist, was in fact one of America's finest illustrators. He was a member of that elite group of artists who have contributed to the highest standards of American illustration—E. A. Abbey, Howard Pyle, N. C. Wyeth, George Luks, George Bellows, John Sloan, Robert Henri, Frank Schoonover, and Charles Dana Gibson, to name but a few.

Many art critics look down their noses at the practitioner who has "prostituted his art" by working in a commercial sphere, particularly that of cartooning. If commercialism be the standard, some of the world's best-known artists would be excluded—Michelangelo, da Vinci, Rubens, Rembrandt, Goya, and a host of others who had to make a living as well as contribute to the artistic genre. Suffice it to say that Foster did his thing, unconcerned as to whether or not he would be considered a true artist by that rarefied group of critics who set contemporary standards only to have them reversed or refined as time changes public attitudes and taste.

Foster was that rare talent who could make a story come alive both in continuity and artwork. His drawings were unexcelled for their vitality, historical accuracy, and beauty. His uncanny ability to "flesh out" drawing-board characters and place them solidly on a realistic and yet picturesque pictorial panorama sets him apart as a modern master of the comic arts. He was an artist in the grand style, even if his work appeared on the comic pages described by the Hearst papers in the early days as "a rainbow of color, a dream of beauty, a wild burst of laughter, and regular hot stuff." While *Prince Valiant* had its humorous and warm moments, it qualified as "a dream of beauty," establishing a style of perfection in the comic pages of America.

Foster began his art career as an illustrator for a mail-order catalogue. While this can be agonizing work in many respects, it gave him an opportunity to draw the human figure in every type of drapery—and like many disagreeable disciplines, was an excellent training ground.

Foster was chosen in the depression years by United Feature Syndicate to illustrate Edgar Rice Burroughs' creation, *Tarzan*. The first pages appeared in 1931, and Foster always considered this feature "a skeleton in the closet." His artistic genius, however, was as evident in *Tarzan* as in the early pages of *Prince Valiant,* but Foster was never proud of *Tarzan,* as he felt he had to "grind it out" in a hurry rather than devote the time he thought necessary to produce a first-rate comic page. Despite his own lack of admiration for his early work, the drawings were dramatic and caught the excitement of the Burroughs script. *Tarzan* was immediately popular with the public and has been a major feature from its inception to the present.

Foster gave up *Tarzan* and created *Prince Valiant* in 1935, combining his interest in history with his expert draftsmanship. It was not in the traditional cartoon style with balloons as dialogue, but was in fact an illustrated novel with the story line lettered at the bottom of the drawings. A stickler for detail, Foster traveled all over the world gathering material for his feature and making intricate sketches which he later incorporated into the body of his work.

I had first met the Fosters in 1940 when they were residents of Evanston, Illinois. I was a kid, wet behind the ears, and had great diffi-

Harold R. "Hal" Foster; *Prince Valiant*—reprinted with special permission of King Features Syndicate, Inc.

"I AM SURE MY WIFE WILL NOT MIND IF I CHARGE YOU A KISS FOR THE RIDE."

1082   11 - 3 - 57

PRINCE VALIANT

A WEIRD, SHADOWY PLACE OF FANTASTIC SHAPES AND BROODING SILENCE..... ALMOST ANYTHING IS MORE THAN LIKELY TO HAPPEN HERE..... VAL HAS THE STRANGE FEELING OF BEING WATCHED!

NEXT WEEK—

The Watcher.

—HAL FOSTER

173   6-2-40

culty in getting from the downtown Chicago hotel where my family was staying to this sub-urban bedroom community. I traveled alone on the train to Evanston and took a taxi to their home. Helen and Hal were like kinfolk, making me feel much at home, although they had never laid eyes on the young stranger from Washington, D.C. I questioned Foster at length about the way he worked, and he kindly brought out his notebooks where he had care-fully laid out sequences of Val in detailed sketches. From this notebook he transferred the text and drawings to Strathmore drawing board, usually breaking up his pages into thirds so that they would fit comfortably on the drawing board. I asked him for an original Sunday page, and I recall his comment. "I keep my originals for book reproduction," he said, "but if you ever get into the business, I will

send you one." I was disappointed, but he explained how important it was to retain the original pages to assure a better image when the drawings were reproduced. His words fell on deaf ears. I had failed in my quest and was heartsick.

I had been with the *News Leader* about six months when one day a large package arrived in the mail. It was an original Sunday page of *Prince Valiant* by Hal Foster. He had selected a sequence which he particularly liked and, true to his word, had forwarded it to me.

Hal and Helen and a number of other artists and wives attended a National Cartoonists Society meeting in Williamsburg, Virginia, a few miles south of the capital city of Richmond while I was with the *News Leader*. Hal and Helen had recently appeared on the Ralph Edwards television show, "This is Your Life,"

SOON THEY ARE HALTED AT THE EDGE OF A GLEN, DOWN WHICH ROARS A FOAMING TORRENT, AND THEIR DREAMS OF AN EASY ROAD THROUGH THE MOUNTAINS FADE. NEXT WEEK:—The Hidden Pass.

Harold R. "Hal" Foster; *Prince Valiant*—reprinted with special permission of King Features Syndicate, Inc.

and he was loaded with photographic equipment which had been given to him on the show. *Prince Valiant* had just been the subject of a major motion picture with Robert Wagner as the prince, Janet Leigh as Aleta, and James Mason as the wicked Black Knight. Foster found it more difficult to make his camera work that he did his brush. He was unfamiliar with the equipment, and it was causing him great discomfort juggling the cameras, light meters, and other paraphernalia about the small reconstructed city. Still he kept clicking pictures of the historic buildings. I was fascinated watching him feel the texture of the bricks with the tips of his fingers.

"What are you doing, Hal?" I asked inquisitively.

"I'm checking the brick," he responded. "Art, did you ever notice how many different types there are in this town? So far, I have spotted about a dozen distinct varieties—some with high straw content, some with practically no straw at all. Fascinating!"

I had never stopped to inspect the brick, but on having it called to my attention I noticed the wide variance in texture and color. Hal hadn't missed a trick or a brick. He had taken it all in.

He also took it all in at a party held for the cartoonists group in Yorktown by one of the town's matriarchs. The gathering was held in a colonial mansion a short distance from the battleground, in an area surrounded by English boxwood. It was a lovely home with formal gardens and brick patios.

Williamsburg, like Richmond, is hot and humid in the summer. That evening the weather was particularly close and oppressive. A butler was making the rounds with a silver tray filling drink orders. The libations being proffered were mint juleps—a popular and potent Southern concoction consisting of powdered sugar, crushed ice, mint, and a full glass of bourbon. Apparently, Hal was not familiar with this old Virginia beverage.

Like most cartoonists, Foster was proficient at holding his liquor, having tifted with the best. But the weather was devastatingly hot and the juleps went down smoothly, one after the other. Hal, in the best Southern tradition, went down, too. He passed out cold between the magnolia and the mint beds. Helen was horrified as they were scheduled to attend a friend's wedding later that evening. Even with all-out effort, Helen was unable to get him to the church on time.

In the late 'fifties, the Fosters moved from Illinois to Redding Ridge, Connecticut, where they had acquired a large Cape Cod home on a lake. The migratory ducks stopped there enroute to their mating grounds. According to Hal, most of the mating was done within earshot. "Those ducks," he remarked with a chuckle, "are better entertainment than anything on TV."

After many years in Connecticut, the Fosters sold their extensive property and headed to Florida where the climate was kinder in the winter, and the ducks quieter.

In the 1960s Hal Foster turned over the drawing of *Prince Valiant* to the talented John Cullen Murphy, illustrator and creator of *Big Ben Bolt,* a sports oriented comic strip. Foster continued to lay out the page, write the text, and color the proofs for the engraver until his death in 1982.

16

Eisenhower Takes a Spill

DWIGHT DAVID EISENHOWER was a military hero, his face known to millions. His beaming smile, his bald head, and his V-for-Victory sign were as familiar as Uncle Sam. My morgue was crammed with photographs of Ike on the battlefield, returning to the U.S., or attending various world conferences. Eisenhower was a great friend of Editor Douglas Southall Freeman, who was one of the first to propose Ike for the presidency. Dr. Freeman had taught the general at the War College and was Ike's close friend. As a consequence, Eisenhower had frequently visited Richmond and even received an honorary degree from the University of Richmond, Freeman's alma mater. At these times, he would always come to the newspaper for lunch in the paneled board room. I had never seen him up close until his campaign trip to Richmond. This was to prove a most eventful time, indeed!

John S. Battle was the Governor of Virginia at the time. He had been with my father in the law firm of Hudson & Cason in Miami during the depression. John Battle had returned to Virginia. It was most helpful being a cartoonist in Richmond with the governor of Virginia as a friend. When I learned Ike was to make a campaign trip to Richmond, I went over to the capitol building to visit Battle. I told him of my desire to meet Ike, and he graciously arranged to have me seated on the platform close to Eisenhower during the political rally. It was decided that the best place for Ike to make his campaign speech would be on the steps of the capitol building. The capitol, designed by Thomas Jefferson, had very steep steps. Special stands were built over the steps so that television cameras could photograph the candidate. The stands were constructed much like the sides of a triangle, with the hypotenuse being the steps of the capitol. I watched as the workmen installed the partitions and framework, and looked forward with great anticipation to being close to the international figure I had seen pictured so often in the world press.

Eisenhower reminded me of the comic character "Henry" drawn by Carl Anderson. He had a shiny bald head and always sported a broad smile. I had done a cartoon of Ike swinging on the Texas Lone Star. Texas was the first state to endorse Eisenhower for the presidency, and I was anxious to have this original cartoon autographed by Ike to hang in my office to go with a cartoon autographed by President Truman. Governor Battle had made plans for me to meet Eisenhower after the speech and to come back to his office so that the general might do the autographing.

The big day finally arrived. The long, black limousine pulled up to the front of Jefferson's

Art Wood; courtesy *Richmond Times-Dispatch/Richmond News Leader*

capitol building and the distinguished general descended from the car, accompanied by the governor of Virginia.

Eisenhower looked quite different in person from the Eisenhower in photographs. He had a ruddy glow. He was a large man, with large features and large hands—the largest hands I have ever seen. He entered the capitol with his wife Mamie and strolled out onto the portico that had been erected over the steps. The large crowd was seated on the ground in the park in front, and rows of gym-type chairs had been placed behind the speaker's podium. Dignitaries from all over the state and, indeed, from all over the country, were on hand. It was a packed crowd both in the park and on the platform.

A rousing cheer greeted Ike as he strolled into public view. The television cameras ground away. I felt fortunate to be standing nearby. There was a tremendous roar from the crowd as he stepped to the microphone. The speech he gave that day was unimpressive, but the crowd received him cordially. At the conclusion of his talk there was wild applause, and even those on the stands began to stamp their feet like fans at a football game. The vibrations of the large crowd caused the stands to shake violently. As Eisenhower walked back from the microphone, the platform under him gave way, and he fell a full fifteen feet to the stone steps below.

I had been told to walk over to meet the general and the governor at the conclusion of the talk and was approaching when the vibrations began. Sen. William Knowland of California was on the other side of Eisenhower as the stands collapsed beneath our feet. I spotted the general at the bottom of the cavernous hole, pulling himself together. I was afraid that he had broken his back. His face was bloody red and he was furious. His first word was, "Where the hell is Mamie?" After being assured that she was safe, with Senator Knowland on one side and the police and myself on the other, General Eisenhower was rescued from what might have been a serious accident. Fortunately, he was not hurt—his heavy cashmere coat broke the fall and

protected him from the impact of the steps. My cartoon, safely tucked beneath my arm as I walked toward the general, had been crushed under the stands. It took the police several days to recover it. Ike was in no mood to sign anything! He felt that there had been a lack of security and that the people who had put the stands together had done a careless job, and he didn't hesitate to say so. Of course, he was swamped by reporters, as well as *Life* photographers and the news wire services. With a politician's tact, he told everyone that he was all right and walked back through the capitol to his car. But he was fighting mad.

The administrative assistant to the governor assured me that the cartoon would be recovered by workmen the next day, but it precluded any opportunity to visit with the general. It was to be a long time after his election as president of the United States before I succeeded in having the original signed. Much upset by the event that had just transpired, I went back to the newspaper office to turn out my daily cartoon. I was in the process of inking the drawing when Hugh Haynie, the associate cartoonist for the *Richmond Times-Dispatch* who filled in for Fred O. Seibel, dashed into my office waving copy from the AP wire.

"My God, Art," he said. "Have you seen what has just come over the teletype?" But I was so busy I hadn't seen anything. He handed me a yellow sheet that had been ripped from the teletype machine. The story with a New York dateline described the Eisenhower accident which had just occurred. Then a paragraph froze my blood. There in cold type it said, "The FBI is investigating the political cartoonist of the *Richmond News Leader* who was spotted earlier in the day at the site of the stands." It stated that cartoonist Art Wood was seen weakening some of the planks undergirding the stands, and went on at length to say that he was "gnawing at the boards and picking away the supports with his pen."

A group of AP staffers then shuffled into my office bent over with laughter. Hugh had "dummied" the fake message on the AP teletype to needle me on my big day with Eisenhower. I still have the copy of the fake teletype message. Looking back, it was very funny, but it wasn't humorous at the time. This gigantic "put on" had achieved its objective, jolting me as nothing has before or since.

Eisenhower eventually invited a select group of cartoonists from the National Cartoonists Society to breakfast. President Eisenhower and Secretary of the Treasury George M. Humphrey appeared informally, and a compilation of drawings was presented to the president. These drawings were later reproduced in a book entitled *President Eisenhower's Cartoon Book by 95 of America's Leading Cartoonists*, with a foreword by Secretary Humphrey. The breakfast was revealing. Eisenhower made a number of special references to cartoons and his interest in the field. He said that he had always avidly followed *Mutt and Jeff*, the comic strip created by Bud Fisher, then being drawn by Al Smith. Al Smith's feature, because of the president's remark, blossomed forth in newspapers all over the world. It was a shot in the arm for both Al and *Mutt and Jeff*. Other artists President Eisenhower said he particularly admired were Chic Young, who drew *Blondie*, and Hal Foster, creator of *Prince Valiant*.

Although President Eisenhower followed the comics, I always had the feeling that he really didn't have much interest in cartooning as such, and I was surprised by his lack of a sense of humor. I had brought along my original cartoon that had disappeared under the stands in Richmond, and all the cartoonists who attended the breakfast signed the crumpled drawing. Bill Holman, who created the comic strip *Smokey Stover*, had also signed the cartoon and had lettered his motto "Foo" prominently across the cartoon. Just for the fun of it, Bill had written his trademark on the president's forehead in the cartoon. Ike stopped cold when he saw the inscription scrawled across his face, and said, "What the hell is that?" I explained to him that Bill Holman used the expression "Foo" as a sort of humorous symbol in his cartoon and had added it as a gag.

"Well, I don't think it's a damn bit funny," Eisenhower replied. And that was that! But he signed the cartoon.

17

The Dynamic
Dynamite Dunn

BACK IN the 1930s and early 1940s, one of the more popular comics was *Joe Jinks*. The strip was originated by Vic Forsythe and continued by Moe Leff and Morris Weiss. The comic featured a prizefighter named Dynamite Dunn and was United Feature Syndicate's effort to simulate Ham Fisher's highly popular *Joe Palooka*.

The most colorful character in the strip was Joe Jinks, a carbon copy of the bald-headed fight promoter, Knobby Walsh, of the Palooka menagerie. Joe was a smooth-talking fast operator whose animated repartee rolled lyrically over his tongue as his fat cigar wobbled from his lower lip. He was typical of the characters that populated the strip. His real-life identical twin was a large burly cartoonist with a jutting jaw and a huge head. An ever-present cigar dangled from his mouth much like that of his comic protege, with billows of thick smoke circling his head like the cloud covering Al Capp's Joe Btfsplk.

The first time I met this "cartoon character" was when King Features executive Brad Kelly took me "downstairs" from his penthouse suite to meet some of the Hearst cartoonists. At that time, Bob (Dynamite) Dunn had an office on the seventeenth floor. He was ghosting Jimmy Hatlo's *They'll Do It Every Time* and was producing a comic of his own, *Just the Type*—a Sunday feature deflating stuffed shirts in a Hatlo-like manner.

He greeted me with a hearty handshake, a billow of cigar smoke in the face, and a voice that shook the hall. Bobo (as he was known to the *King* staff) was a cartoonist's cartoonist. He had worked with Milt Gross on *That's My Pop* and was the production manager of the team that turned out the Hatlo feature. Bobo was a jack of all trades—a superior cartoonist, an effective radio commentator, a hysterical master of ceremonies, raconteur, and all-around cut-up. Most cartoonists drawing funny features are serious, but Bobo was hilarious in person as in his work. His good humor was as contagious as the mumps and funny—until it dropped. He had a disarming way of putting you at ease and then carefully setting you up for a variety of practical jokes.

In my *News Leader* days I was as poor as a church mouse, but whenever I was in the New York area Bobo treated me like a visiting celebrity.

My wife's family summer home was near Greenwich, Connecticut, and it was necessary to rise at dawn in order to reach the city by business hours. On one trip I drove through the country to the subway station, parked my car, and then caught the train into crowded Grand Central Station. My breakfast consisted of a small glass of juice and a gulped cup of coffee. As lunchtime approached I was ravenous.

"You must have lunch with me at the Palm," Bobo had told me that morning, and of course I was delighted to accept. It proved, however, to be a very long lunch hour. The Palm was a well-known New York watering place right around the corner from King Features on Second Avenue. It was an oasis in a desert of skyscrapers and a hangout for theatre people. Large fans rotated on the ceiling and sawdust covered the floor. It resembled a British tavern both in architecture and in atmosphere.

The pub was attractively decorated with cartoons by most of the famous men in the field. Some were framed, but most were drawn right on the wall. Over the years the plaster had yellowed so that many of the drawings were obscure and faded. I particularly recall the drawings of Robert L. Ripley, Hal Foster, Alex Raymond, and Milton Caniff, all of whom apparently had doodled on the wall in pen-and-ink or watercolor for the price of a drink or dinner. It was a rogues' gallery of graphic masters.

The bar was on one side of the room, and by far the more populated spot. The restaurant, specializing in rare roast beef, was on the other side, separated by a column of wooden see-through stakes. Our first stop, however, was not on the restaurant side.

We crowded into the bar. On hand were such illustrious figures as Harry Hershfield, Joe Musial, Paul Frehm, Dave Breger, Milton Caniff, and a host of lesser lights, public relations executives, and newspaper editors.

Feeling self-conscious and anxious to be one of the group, I took out my wallet to buy Bobo a drink. He exploded in the loudest announcement I had heard since my cheerleading days in high school. "Drinks on Wood!" he roared, his deep, resonant voice echoing throughout the small two-room restaurant. With that, the restaurant, which was by then full of people, also exploded. It was Grand Central Station all over again. Everyone raced to the bar. I had a five-dollar bill which I had hoped would cover both drinks. When I saw the mass of humanity wrapped around the bar I froze in confusion and panic. As quickly as they gathered, however, they dispersed. It was a ruse to scare "first nighters," and it worked like a charm. The entire restaurant chuckled at my discom-

fort, and then I laughed as loudly as any of them. It was one of Bobo Dunn's practical jokes—the mildest I was to experience at his hands over the years.

At the table, he introduced me to the celebrated newspaper men as "Art Wood, an insurance agent from Washington." I cringed, but after they discovered I was another cartoonist, the ice was broken.

I particularly remember the noted humorist and creator of *Abie the Agent*, Harry Hershfield, who had just returned from a trip to Washington where he had stopped by the White House to see his old friend Ike. "You know," he mused, lowering his voice as if he were disclosing some national defense secret, "Ike likes a dirty joke as much as anybody I know, but he always cleans things up for the public. He can out cuss Patton," he explained, "but Mamie does not like off-color language or stories, so he is very careful what he does and says. But he always looks forward to a new raunchy story and I always have one for him," Hershfield added. Then he related a dozen or so typical stories. We were entranced. One story led to another and with contributions by one and all, the already late luncheon extended far into the afternoon.

I was astounded at how the cartoonists could down double martinis and then go back to the office for an afternoon of work. "Amazing group, these New York cartoonists," I thought to myself.

On another trip to New York I got a special dose of Dynamite Dunn! It was summer and a typical hot, rainy day. I came equipped with a raincoat, which was hung on the antique hatrack behind Bobo Dunn's cluttered office door. Papers were strewn all over the room, proofs of Sunday pages were stacked knee-deep in the corner, and Bobo was slouched in his favorite nook near the telephone where numbers were scribbled on the wall from just above the floor board all the way to the ceiling. Everyone from Joan Crawford to Bishop Sheen was listed.

Bobo was sitting crosslegged in front of his drawing board, roughing out his cartoon on bond paper and clutching the ever present

They'll Do It Every Time-:- By JIMMY HATLO

Jimmy Hatlo; *They'll Do It Every Time*—reprinted with special permission of King Features Syndicate, Inc.

cigar in his brown-stained fingers. "You are just in time for lunch," he said, although it was barely 11:15. He put out his cigar and adjusted his tie, grabbing his coat from the same rack housing my tattered raincoat. "The restaurant is just across the street, so I won't wear my overcoat," he advised. So away we went down the long corridor to the elevator. As we got on at the seventeenth floor, I noticed a blonde, beautifully dressed, with a low-cut beige blouse and matching umbrella among the group in the elevator. She was a lovely girl, probably a model posing for newspaper advertisements.

The elevator was crowded and as the door closed, Bobo Dunn gave her a hard pinch on the fanny, admonishing me in a loud stern voice, "Arthur, in the big city we don't do things like that!" The girl, thinking I had been the one to get fresh in the elevator, began to pummel me with her umbrella and continued striking me in the head and back until the elevator mercifully reached the lobby. Everyone in the elevator thought I was the culprit and there was much flurry and indignation. It was no use trying to explain. I made a quick exit onto 45th Street toward Second Avenue as Bobo Dunn doubled up in laughter. My head was sore for a week.

Ironically, the worst gag he pulled on me was unintentional. Jimmy Hatlo used to acknowledge ideas sent in for *They'll Do It Every Time*

Bob "Bobo" Dunn; *Just the Type*—reprinted with special permission of King Features Syndicate, Inc.

with a "tip of the Hatlo hat." The credit was usually tucked away in a box at the bottom corner of the panel. Since Bobo ghosted the panel, he filled in the names of the contributors. Sometimes, if the letter was unsigned, Bobo would stick in the name of friends to fill the space. He asked me one time at lunch if he could use my name occasionally in the credit box. Of course, I was flattered that he wanted to do so and gave a quick okay.

In Richmond, the Hatlo panel was used by the paper "across the aisle"—the morning *Richmond Times-Dispatch*. The cartoon appeared on the op-ed page across from the editorial cartoon and was prominently featured at the top. One day one of my friends called up, convulsed with laughter. "Did you see your name in Hatlo's panel today?" he chortled. "It is a killer. Funniest damn cartoon I ever saw, and I understand the managing editor of your paper is fuming." The idea, which was not my own but Bobo Dunn's, involved a newspaper editor who visualized himself as the great American novelist. The drawing depicted the editor pecking away on a

battered typewriter with a stack of rejection slips on the desk, and with all the office force making comments behind his back at the rear of the cartoon. It carried such gems as: "There goes Gasket, starting on the great American novel again. Whenever he does that, it means the pony-boys are taking him to the cleaners." "He can't write a news story in less than ten paragraphs . . . but he can't get past the title on that book." "Been writing it six years . . . the only way he'll make any dough is to sell that scrap paper on the floor."

Unknown to me, both the editor and managing editor of my paper had been trying to peddle outside pieces to *Reader's Digest* and other publications to supplement their income; to date, they had been unsuccessful. So it hit the fan. They thought I was attempting to satirize their situation and were incensed.

It took some time to rectify the mixup. I still think they thought I was trying to "turn the knife" when in fact I was just getting the dynamic Dynamite Dunn treatment—and innocently at that.

18

A Fine Line

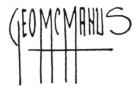

GEORGE MCMANUS, who made corned beef and cabbage and the rolling pin famous, was one of the few cartoonists to look exactly like his creation. He was the spitting image of Jiggs. His face was as fluid as the map of Ireland, and his ever-present cigar billowed clouds of white smoke to dry the ink from the carefully penned comic characters who populated *Bringing Up Father*. McManus was Jiggs, and Jiggs was McManus.

The three McManus brothers looked very much alike but were quite different in personality. Leo was the crotchety brother who ran the King Features stable in New York, while his more even-dispositioned brother drew his comic from Beverly Hills. The third brother, Charles, was an off-and-on cartoonist drawing in the same style as his brother George.

George McManus traveled to New York for parties and contract-signing, but worked from a palatial studio at his California home. He was a special favorite of publisher William Randolph Hearst and turned out a number of features over the years, including *Panhandle Pete, Spareribs and Gravy, The Newlyweds, Rosie's Beau, Let George Do It, Their Only Child,* and *The Whole Blooming Family*. He began work on his famous comic *Bringing Up Father* in 1913 and continued drawing the feature until his death in 1954.

McManus was one of the most skillful, facile, and decorative of all the early comic artists. He had a natural sense of design and pattern which gave his drawings a beauty rarely seen in the early comic pages, which were often crudely put together. In the initial stages of the comic strip, the idea usually carried the cartoon, with a minimum of time being spent on artwork. McManus' sense of

BRINGING UP FATHER

George McManus; *Bringing Up Father*—reprinted with special permission of King Features Syndicate, Inc.

109

perspective and architectural composition, however, gave his originals depth and an illustrational quality. His fine pen lines flowed with rapidity and ease. He rarely pencilled his drawings. He knew just how to treat the figure and to spot his black areas for maximum effect. His comic was a superb blend of art and script. The text was hilarious, and the artwork enhanced the story line.

McManus was a poor correspondent. I had written to him, drawn special sketches asking for an original, and even enlisted his own characters to appeal to his ego, but with no result. I wrote him regularly for two or three

SPARERIBS AND GRAVY

George McManus; *Spareribs & Gravy*—reprinted with special permission of King Features Syndicate, Inc.

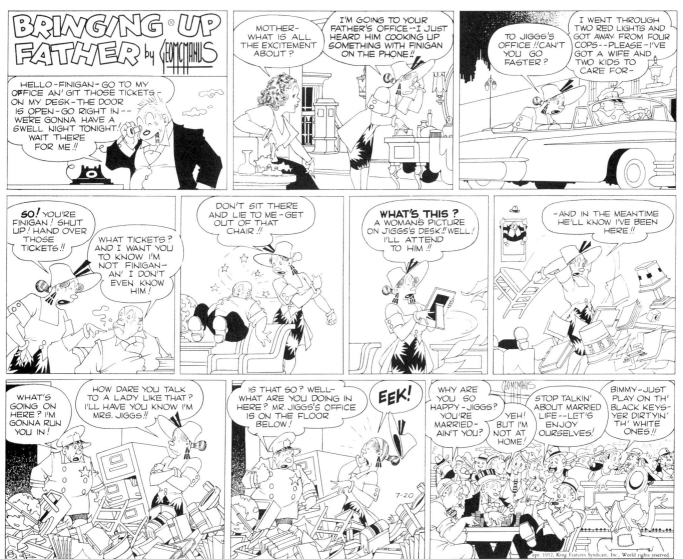

George McManus; *Bringing Up Father*—reprinted with special permission of King Features Syndicate, Inc.

years. Finally, one day an original comic strip arrived in the mail, wrapped in toilet-roll cardboard. The drawing had been mashed to shreds enroute, and I was as crushed as the original. I placed it under a number of volumes of the *Encyclopedia Britannica* in an attempt to flatten it, but to no avail. It still showed the folds and ridges caused by a careless post office. So I rolled out an ironing board and heated up a flat iron. With great care I pressed out the 1939 original. As luck would have it, the pressure on the drawing scorched the paper, burning it a rusty brown. I was heart-broken. I sat down and wrote McManus another long letter explaining my ordeal and asking for a substitute original to frame for my room. He never replied. It was a number of years before I was able to obtain another original McManus drawing.

In the middle 1950s, McManus became ill. Zeke Zekely, a well-known West Coast cartoonist, assisted him with the strip. As McManus became more seriously ill, his old daily and Sunday cartoons were cut apart and cleverly reassembled with new story lines and gags. The originals were patched together like a crossword puzzle. Styles and hairdos in the old drawings were updated and modernized,

and the comic retained its humor and appeal. Only the engraver knew of their true origin.

When McManus passed away late in 1954, the syndicate faced the problem of finding a new artist to draw the strip. For some reason Zekely was passed over. Other King Features artists were considered, and a few, including the talented Bob Naylor, drew special strips in the McManus style for the syndicate executives to consider. The man finally selected to do the daily was a splendid choice. Vernon Greene, a former political cartoonist for the *Portland Oregonian,* had ghosted a number of top King strips—including *The Shadow* and *Polly and Her Pals.* He copied the McManus line so skillfully that only an expert could have detected a difference.

His method was simple but effective. He employed a light board, a drawing board with a glass plate instead of the usual wood surface. A light beneath the glass enabled the artist to see through his drawing paper and carefully duplicate anything traced on the paper. Greene requested every available McManus original from the syndicate files, which he used for reference. In his initial efforts to emulate the master, the drawings were copied with great care and exactitude. It was a perfect imitation of the creator's style and fine line. As Vernon became more familiar with McManus' technique, the drawings became freer and,

although rendered in McManus' style, were not as intricate or precise.

Vernon lived in a farmhouse in Wyckoff, New Jersey. His attractive colonial home was situated close by a large barn which he transformed into a joint office/studio with drawing board, desk, filing cabinets, and air conditioning. Vernon was a pack rat and a photography enthusiast, and a good portion of the spare space was stacked with enlargers, cameras, and photographic gear. The McManus originals were filed carefully in large brown envelopes by year—the dailies in one place and the Sundays in another. He was very organized, and everything had its proper place.

Vernon bubbled with personality and enthusiasm for the trade. He was tall and curly headed and looked much younger than his age. He was married to a statuesque redhead named Rusty—a second marriage for them both—and the house was crowded with attractive sons and daughters. Vernon had the milk of human kindness as well as India ink flowing in his veins. He was the epitome of the Christian gentleman—thoughtful, unselfish, and gracious. He enjoyed people, and they enjoyed him. He drew the McManus feature more for love than money, and in order to supplement his salary he did radio interviews and television spots. Frank Fletcher, another King

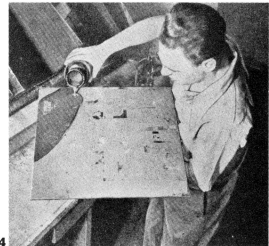

3

4

It is an elaborate process that takes a cartoon from the drawing board to a newspaper page. The late George McManus, creator of "Bringing Up Father," signs (1) a finished drawing. A print is then colored (2) to serve as a guide for the engravers (3) who photograph the original on a glass plate (4). Using the colored print as a guide, the plate is shaded (5). After etching, Jiggs comes to life in a sample copy (6) printed by hand. Cardboard-like impressions are made from the finished plates. For offset printing, a velox copy is sent to newspapers. Presses roll (7).

5

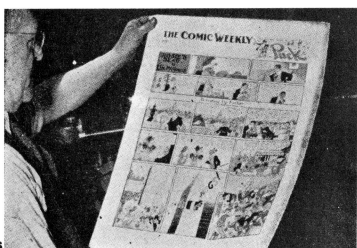

6

7

Photos of George McManus at work; courtesy Art Wood collection

BRINGING UP FATHER

Features artist, produced the Sunday *Bringing Up Father* in conjunction with writer/editor Bill Kavanagh.

Vernon was a good samaritan in modern dress. He visited the sick, encouraged the downtrodden, and was always there with a cheerful word and an open pocketbook. Few of his friends knew the time and effort he spent in helping the indigent. A case in point was his friendship with Charlie Payne.

Charles Payne was at one time one of the most famous cartoonists in the country, with a widely read feature called *S'Matter Pop*. Born in 1873, Charlie had come from sturdy colonial stock. His Scotch-Irish ancestors were from western Ohio and Pennsylvania. The Steeles on his grandfather's side were British-Swiss, and Colonel Crawford on his grandmother's side had served as George Washington's guide and land agent. Crawford, according to Charlie, was burned at the stake by Indians on the present site of Crawfordsville, Ohio. Young Charlie, when he was eight, decided to become an astronomer while attending a one-room country school house. He lived out in the country where an old apple tree with woodpecker holes served as the post office. He liked to sketch. When a neighbor encouraged him to go to the big city to sell his drawings, instead of mailing them to local newspapers he forgot astronomy. He gravitated to Pittsburgh where he obtained a job as bellboy at the prestigious Duquesne Club. In his spare time he submitted cartoon ideas to the *Pittsburgh Post*. He eventually joined the paper to produce a front-page political cartoon. After a stint at editorial cartoons, he discovered the grass (and paychecks) were greener in the comics, and so he launched his strip. It was a popular feature for a number of years, and Charlie Payne became a wealthy man, even able to afford membership in the Duquesne Club with Carnegie and

S'MATTER POP

Charles Payne; *S'Matter Pop*—courtesy Bell Syndicate

Mellon. In the early 1900s he moved to New York into a spacious apartment on the west side. As the years passed, his feature waned in popularity and Charlie came upon hard times. His fortune dried up, and he was left with only the apartment and his memories. The area where he lived gradually deteriorated, but like so many people, Charlie preferred to remain in familiar quarters, despite the shabby surroundings and ever-present danger.

Vernon Greene took a special interest in the old cartoonist and tried to persuade him to move to a safer locale, but it was a hopeless attempt. Charlie was unable to sever his ties with the past. Vernon decided the next best thing was to make the old man as comfortable as possible in his limited quarters. He gave Charlie a radio to occupy his time and a typewriter to answer his infrequent correspondence. He also visited the apartment every week and handled the old fellow's financial obligations.

Whenever I was in New York, I also went to visit Charlie. He was at that time in his nineties. The door to his westside apartment was bolted with locks from the floor to the ceiling. It took Charlie an endless time to remove the chains and get the door open. Payne was thin and frail but still well-dressed and neat, with flowing white hair and a cravat about his neck.

After one extended visit he said to me, "You and Vernon have been so kind to me I am going to make you both millionaires. Some years ago I uncovered a cache of meteorites near Poughkeepsie, New York. I have hidden these meteorites so no one can find them and have arranged for a firm in Puerto Rico to cut the rocks into one-eighth-inch pieces for setting in costume jewelry. With the interest in the space age, I can make a fortune, and you will be the benefactors for what you have done for me. I am the only one who knows the hiding place," he whispered.

Charlie was never able to reveal his secret. One night on the elevator in his delapidated building a burly hoodlum beat the fragile little

BRINGING UP FATHER

George McManus; *Bringing Up Father*—reprinted with special permission of King Features Syndicate, Inc.

BRINGING UP FATHER

George McManus; *Bringing Up Father*—reprinted with special permission of King Features Syndicate, Inc.

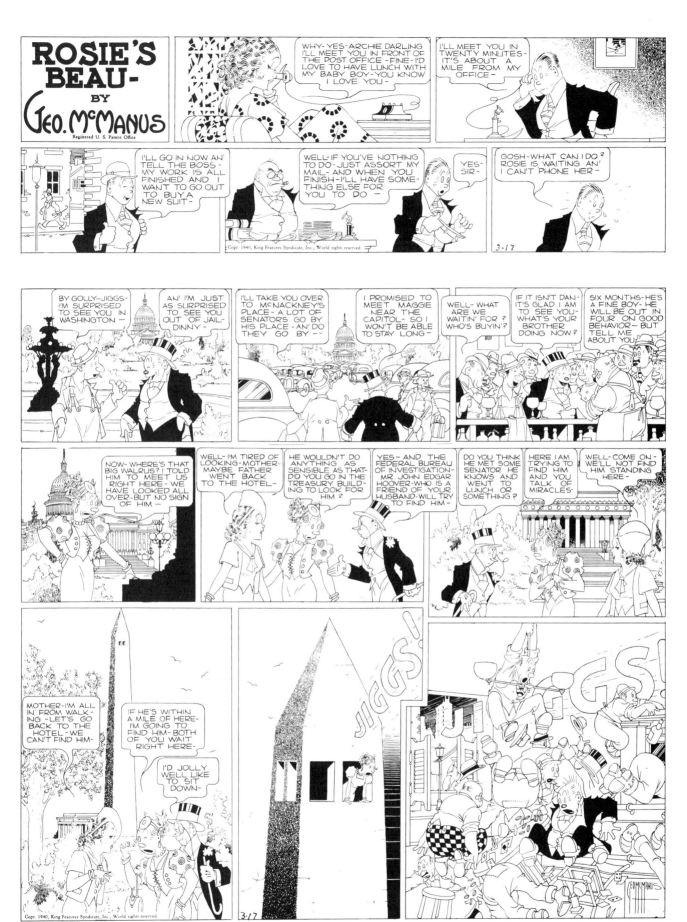

George McManus; *Rosie's Beau*—reprinted with special permission of King Features Syndicate, Inc.

man into unconsciousness for the few cents he had in his pocket. Payne's jaw was broken in four places, and he was crippled. The old man died soon after.

Vernon Greene paid all of Charlie's hospital fees and financed the funeral. No one knew of Vernon's generosity, and I only found out after Vernon himself passed away. Vernon's death closely followed that of Payne. He died of cancer in 1957. After his death, I was able to obtain Vernon's collection of original drawings, both his own work and the remaining originals by George McManus. The fine line was unbroken.

BRINGING UP FATHER

George McManus; *Bringing Up Father*—reprinted with special permission of King Features Syndicate, Inc.

19

The Vim and Dash of Zim

EUGENE ZIMMERMAN, a pen-and-ink humorist of rare aptitude and distinction, used the pen name "Zim." His drawings captured the mood and flavor of rural America at its best—and, in addition, they were extremely funny to look at.

His work influenced many of the top practitioners who followed him. He took careful aim at America's diverse ethnic groups and

ZIMMERMAN SELF-PORTRAIT

Eugene "Zim" Zimmerman; *Puck* magazine

humorously depicted the hayseed farmer, the Irish hod carrier, the German storekeeper, the black laborer, the pipestove rube, and the city slicker, but he always drew in a sympathetic and loving manner while poking fun at all phases of the small-town life he knew so well.

Zim was from a little hamlet in the lake country of New York—Horseheads—so named because during a skirmish with the Indians, the early settlers had cut off the heads of captured Indian stallions, following the style of Elizabethan England, and had impaled the heads as a warning to the Indians of dire consequences to come. The horses' heads must have scared off more than the Indians, for Horseheads was and is a thinly populated town.

Zim was fiercely loyal to this section of the country, and especially to his hometown and Chemung County, so rich in early American history. Zim described Horseheads as follows in his cartoon course:

> As for our climate, Florida has nothing on us. We stand high and dry, thank goodness, and we have defied the floods and tempests of a hundred years or more. When other localities were rent asunder by the elements, not even a Horseheads gooseberry has been shaken from its mooring. When our present firm of undertakers started business here, they purchased the "dead" stock of a discouraged embalmer who found our town too

healthy and unprofitable. It was a bad risk and for two years following the aforesaid purchase, the present firm was so desperately in need of business that some of our aged settlers, out of pure sympathy, volunteered to cash in their chips, which custom is strictly observed to this day, for every community must maintain an undertaker, even if it calls for an occasional sacrifice. These conditions are due solely to our balmy atmosphere. Then again, where would you find a city along whose trolley tracks may be plucked on any dewy Sunday morning luscious mushrooms, and where people repose such confidence in one another that they retire to their homes leaving their places of business unlocked and the sign of welcome upon their safes: 'unlocked, use no dynamite.' These and numerous other features, original with us only, place us in a decidedly distinct position against the world at large. . . . There's no doubt about it that Horseheads was originally selected as the most suitable site for the garden of Eden; but, for some slight misunderstanding on the part of those who had the matter in charge, they

Eugen

Eugene "Zim" Zimmerman; *Puck* magazine

evidently got mixed on their maps, for here we had all the required stage settings for this beautiful drama—the snakes, the apple trees, and the balmy atmosphere.

Zim's brown gingerbread house still stands a block or so from the city square, which boasts a plaque and a bandstand honoring the village's most noted citizen. His only daughter Laura lived in the Victorian home until her death and kept it much the same as when Zim was alive.

Zim, like so many artists of the early 1900s, worked at an old roll-top desk at the back of his parlor where he juggled a bread board in his lap, propped against the desk. Here he drew his funny pictures with a pen and brush or crayon, occasionally rendering an original in wash or color. He was a pleasant, fun-loving person who sketched constantly and worked fast.

Beginning as an apprentice to a sign painter, he had trained with a number of noted artists, including Bernard Gillam and the senior Joseph Keppler, founder and editor of *Puck* magazine. Zim described his early days as follows:

> When I began my duties at the *Puck* office, I was obliged to practice a great deal upon lithographic stone before my hand became accustomed to the handling of the litho crayon upon a stone surface. I was then allowed to fill in flat tints for both Mr. Keppler and Mr. Gillam upon their colored stones. This was no difficult task, except to a novice, and it was interesting to note the results (when all three tint stones were on the presses) of the harmonious blending of colors with which the cartoons were illuminated.
>
> Lithographic crayons are of a soft greasy black substance that must be handled gently, and a lithographic stone has a very finely grained surface which must also be treated with utmost care and cleanliness. By close attention I succeeded in getting fairly even tints so that I assisted Mr. Keppler every week in one way or another. I kept his work table and tools in order. *Puck* was then located at 21 Warren Street, New York, and our studios were on the third floor, overlooking Murray Street. There was nothing pretentious about the place that would indicate that it was the workshop of the great Keppler. The low partitions divided that end of the room into three stalls of about ten to twelve feet each. No pictures or drapery adorned the walls of these compartments— nothing but drawing tables and tools— always immaculately clean, dustless, and ready for business.

Zim's people were true-to-life, but exaggerated to emphasize the weak points of human nature. His farmers were kindly but seedy, his Irishmen fiery but funny, his Negroes hilarious, as were other racial groups drawn to poke fun at their idiosyncrasies. There was, however, nothing mean in Zim's work. He observed his countrymen and drew them with facility and fidelity, but always with charm and good humor.

He worked on the art staff of *Puck* magazine from 1883 to 1886. He then joined the art department of *Judge* magazine where he continued to draw cartoons both humorous and political for twenty-five years. He also contributed to numerous other magazines and periodicals. For many years, under the pseudonym "Ea-Zy Picking, The Rustling Reporter," he conducted a popular column of comments on local and national events in the *Chemung Valley Reporter*.

Zim's work influenced a generation of artists who followed his style and instruction. For not only did he turn out an enormous amount of work, but he also conducted a correspondence school on cartooning from his home in Horseheads.

Unlike many courses of the time, it was well-written, entertaining, and instructive. He did not promise his students quick success and vast fortunes. He just taught them how to draw and showed them the successful techniques he had discovered after years of practice and agonizing trial and error. Zim was careful to emphasize the importance of detail in cartooning, particularly the drawing of hands and feet.

Eugene "Zim" Zimmerman; *Puck* magazine

Here is a typical comment from his course:

> In my lessons I shall teach you to make hands and feet that talk, for I believe there is as much expression in the hand and foot as there is in a face. Many professional artists overlook this part of the human anatomy, and yet in comic drawing and cartooning it is often one of the most important and conspicuous features in a picture.

Zim offered two books a month and personally criticized the drawings and corrected the students' work—a massive undertaking for one man, particularly one so prolific as Zim. He also offered practical tips on how to be happy and get the most out of life. The course included large doses of homespun philosophy spiced with motivational drawing instruction.

Zim kept a tight schedule and felt the best time of the day for creative efforts was the morning.

> For many years, I'd adhere to a system of dividing my working hours from those which I call play hours. I arise early (seldom do I remain in bed past 6:30 A.M.). I go to my desk and work until eight, breakfast, and work again till 10 A.M. The rest of the day I tend to other duties not strictly in the newspaper line. After tea, I again sit down to work and in some instances work until 11 P.M. More often, however, till 8:30, then retire, and usually I feel sufficiently fatigued to welcome sleep without rocking or a lullaby. Of course, I do not keep up this pace every day, as circumstances may alter my daily routine now and then, but I find morning the time to do your best work. The mind is clear and better calculated to grasp problems and work them out.
>
> Very often I make all of my layouts (should I have half a dozen pictures to make) in the morning, and after supper I do the inking (the penwork). The real headwork is in the composition or first layout. The inking is comparatively easy and does not require much mental exertion.

In commenting on his contemporaries, Zim observed,

> Various artists, whose work I noted in some of the country's newspapers, show more creative ability than art talent. They've learned to draw in a mechanical sort of way, every figure having a studied appearance, with garments tediously modeled in fine lines

Eugene "Zim" Zimmerman; *Puck magazine*

and utterly destitute of vim or dash or the strength which is essential in a cartoon to make it a powerful factor and interesting. Some of these men will never draw otherwise because they know not how to improve their style. Most artists who have acquired fame succeeded by constantly improving their technique. That is what I shall expect of my students when they become masters of themselves. Create a technique which will carry your name to the foremost rank of cartoonists. Time will bring about these conditions if you will persevere. It is well to copy others while you are learning, but when you have blossomed out as a contributor to publications, you should cease copying and become an originator.

Zim's work was never destitute of vim or dash, and his strength was making a cartoon

Eugene "Zim" Zimmerman; *Puck* magazine

powerful, interesting, and, perhaps most important, funny.

Zim was a kindly man and a collector's patron saint. In his Course III he had this word of advice for the comic artist:

> There is an obligation you owe your friends and acquaintances, as well as an appreciative public, who admire your productions and desire to possess a slight example of your clever work, which, in token of their friendship and appreciation of your skill, they carefully preserve in a frame or book. Therefore, when a request is made of you (which in the course of time will be the case, as you become known in hundreds of homes) for an autographed sketch in pen and ink or pencil, or even in colors, submit cheerfully by all means, as these favors are highly prized, particularly as they come direct from the artist and are especially made for the person seeking them. Such favors cost you but little time and exertion, and the return is tenfold in many ways, whereas a refusal has a tendency to make you unpopular. Be agreeable and willing to sacrifice the few minutes it would consume to please those who might eventually be the making of you.

> An artist in my early acquaintance once remarked that he never responded to such requests without some compensation, and I have reason to believe that he kept his word. For the fellow has grown rich by his drawing and charging, but I never heard any favorable comment regarding his professional generosity.

Zim's daughter Laura was a close friend, and I was able to obtain the bulk of Zim's original work for my collection. This includes many pages of drawings from his cartoon course and a number of originals from his personal collection.

20

Snap, Crackle, and Pop

VERNON GRANT, a Nebraskan by birth and a New Yorker much of his life, retired in the 'forties to the gracious living of a country squire in the lovely little Southern town of Rock Hill, South Carolina. For years he had been one of the most renowned advertising artists and magazine illustrators in America. But, unlike many of his fellows, Grant foresaw the demise of the general circulation magazines because of the impact of TV, and bowed out of the art scene while he was still on top. Although Vernon Grant had produced covers for *Judge, Ladies Home Journal, Liberty, Colliers,* and other major magazines for years, he is best known for a series of Mother Goose drawings he did for the Kellogg's Company in Battle Creek, Michigan. In addition, he had created the "Snap, Crackle, and Pop" characters to symbolize the freshness of the company's Rice Krispies product.

His work was widely imitated, but never emulated. His style was distinctive and influenced such diverse artisans as Walt Disney, Russell Patterson, Don Flowers, and Walt Scott in this country. His drawings also influenced Antonio Arias Bernal, one of Mexico's leading caricaturists. He had a gift for color and his vivid poster-like paintings decorated children's rooms (and adults', too) around the world.

He was one of the early innovators to use his drawings as decals for promotional purposes.

His cartoons were glazed on plates, drinking glasses, mugs, and window panes, and color reprints of his work were distributed by Kellogg's to fill thousands of requests coast to coast. It was a happy arrangement for both Kellogg's and Grant, and for years he was the primary artist for the company until a dispute regarding reprint rights caused a breakdown in relations and lawsuits followed. This soured

Vernon Grant—reprinted by permission of Grant family

127

the winning combination and ended the use of Grant's drawings on Kellogg's promotions and boxtops.

Grant had a genuis for crisp, imaginative characterizations and rarely since Arthur Rackham, the British illustrator, has anyone captured the elusive quality of youth as well as this talented artist did. He worked very large in tempera on illustration board, and his drawings jumped from the picture. Grant utilized a technique of cutting off the sharp edges of his brush line with Chinese white to give a woodcut-like appearance. His use of S design—a graceful arrangement of the composition in the shape of an S—and careful layout captured an entire scene as if viewed from above or beyond the frame, while at the same time involving the reader in the action of the drawing. His elf-like people were appealing and retained enough realism to give them personality and character.

Grant, although retired, was never able to rest on past accomplishments. He became involved in civic work and headed the Rock Hill Chamber of Commerce. In this position he helped re-develop the city and transform its park areas into major tourist attractions. He designed local public relations folders, and his spot drawings featured in colorful pamphlets were eye-catching and helped promote the community's scenic surroundings. In addition, he still turns out a number of paintings each year for commercial purposes or for his own pleasure.

His home borders a spacious golf course, and he owns considerable property in the vicinity. A shrewd businessman, he had taken what he had made in his heyday and invested in real estate on the eastern shore of Maryland and in the Carolinas. He enjoys the life of a gentleman farmer, and in his spare time devotes himself to cabinet-making and woodwork. Grant is a large burly man. Pudgy, but fit, he sits by his drawing board puffing on a pipe like a latter-day Rip Van Winkle. His eyes twinkle and he enjoys describing his early days as an illustrator and his many artist friends of yesteryear.

His hand remains steady and sure and he keeps a tight schedule, despite the demands of overseeing his "southern plantation." Even in his late seventies, he has an abundance of snap, crackle, and pop!

Vernon Grant—reprinted by permission of Grant family

21

Milton Caniff
GENIAL GENIUS

WHEN THE definitive history of the comics is finally written, standing at the head of the line exchanging a brush for Father Time's quill pen will be a genial genius among comic artists, Milton A. Caniff. Caniff is a pacesetter in the illustrative action strip. His creations, *Terry and the Pirates, Male Call,* and *Steve Canyon,* have been copied in style and technique by a host of artists since he began working for the Associated Press in 1932.

A list of those influenced by Milt reads like a Who's Who of comicdom: Alfred Andriola (*Kerry Drake*), Art Sansone (*Born Loser* and *Chris Welkin*), Mel Graef (*Secret Agent X-9*), Ray Bailey (*Space Patrol*), Rick Fletcher (*Old Glory* and *Dick Tracy*), Frank Robbins (*Johnny Hazard*), and Charles Raab (*Adventures of Patsy*).

Caniff himself was early influenced by Billy Ireland, the editorial cartoonist of the *Columbus Dispatch.* Caniff and several other noted cartoonists got their start on this widely read Midwestern newspaper. Ireland, like many of the political cartoonists of his day, worked with fine cross-hatch pen strokes and was widely imitated by political cartoonists of mid-America.

Caniff's first drawings for the AP were rendered in a pen-and-ink style much like that of his idol Billy Ireland. His good friend and fellow artist at the Associated Press, Noel

Sickles, also drew in a similar technique. Both were soon to give up the pen for the brush and a new approach to the adventure strip.

Caniff and Sickles shared desks in the AP bullpen in Rockefeller Center where the opportunity for budding artists to have their work seen was great, but the pay was poor. Another "cellmate" was Al Capp. Capp, who was just getting underway in the business, was working on a forgettable feature entitled *Colonel*

Milton Caniff; *The Gay Thirties*—courtesy The Associated Press

Milton Caniff; *Dickie Dare*—courtesy The Associated Press

Gilfeather, which he had inherited from another artist.

Milton Caniff, after a stint at retouching, drawing maps, and producing a series of political portraits, was assigned to illustrate a one-column panel called *Puffy the Pig. Puffy* appeared in the morning papers and was a big seller. The feature was so successful that the AP decided to develop a similar one for evening dailies. Caniff designed a strip instead of a panel and sold the syndicate his creation, *Dickie Dare,* a tow-headed kid with a dog and a

dashing older companion, Dan Flynn, probably modeled after a movie star with a similar name. In this strip an idea germinated that would develop into *Terry and the Pirates,* a comic also featuring a youngster with an older sidekick.

Caniff was an innovator, and he quickly switched from his intricate and sometimes crowded pen-and-ink panels of *Dickie Dare* to a greater emphasis on action and dramatic spotting. He used a brush with rich blacks to heighten the mood and transport the reader's eye rapidly through the sequence. Black-and-white spotting and clever layout became Caniff's trademark. He eliminated all unnecessary detail, and his strong, bold brush strokes contrasted with a splendid use of white space. Caniff had reintroduced impressionism to the comics. Lyonel Feininger, George Herriman, and Cliff Sterrett had set the pace, but it remained for Caniff to make style, design, and sophisticated dialogue the key ingredients of the comics.

Like Orson Welles in *Citizen Kane*, he utilized motion-picture techniques to enhance the action of his comic strip—closeup, then a distant shot, a view from above, and a socko ending! Unhappily, the newspaper reduction of the comics today has greatly diminished the effect of such drawing skills. With space reduced to postage-stamp size, the illustrator must resort to closeups and trickery to advance his continuity.

Caniff has always been a demon for detail and research. When he switched drawing boards in 1944 from the AP to the *Chicago*

DICKIE DARE

Milton Caniff; *Dickie Dare*—courtesy The Associated Press

TERRY AND THE PIRATES

Tribune's New York News Syndicate to develop his famous *Terry and the Pirates* comic, he was completely unfamiliar with the Far East locale where the strip was to take place. He had not traveled abroad and had to resort to the New York City Library, the *Encyclopedia Britannica,* authoress Pearl Buck, a stack of books on the Orient, and materials supplied to him by newspaper friends who had been to China. His product, however, was so exact and authentic that even China experts thought they recognized familiar spots and sights. Milt has always done his homework, whether drawing a Chinese junk or

TERRY AND THE PIRATES

Milton Caniff; *Terry & The Pirates*—reprinted by permission: Tribune Media Services

the latest jet. Every plank and bolt is accurately depicted. He has a photograph file that is unmatched. Few libraries can rival it. Over the years he has used models for his characters,

drawing from life as well and as expertly as from his extensive morgue. Each face is selected to most accurately depict the character created. Such celebrities as John F.

Kennedy (Pipper the Piper), Marilyn Monroe (Miss Mizzou), Bill Mauldin (Mr. Bucket), Ilona Massey (Madam Lynx), and Joan Crawford (the Dragon Lady) have been used as models.

And his girls—from the sexy Dragon Lady to the demure April Kane of *Terry and the Pirates*; from the sultry Copper Calhoun or the girl around the corner, Miz Mizzou of *Steve Canyon*—each has a personality as well as generous

MISS LACE

physical charms. Perhaps *Male Call,* which he drew briefly during World War II for *Stars and Stripes,* was Caniff at his pin-up best. His drawings were reprinted and admired by G.I.'s and generals alike around the world.

Caniff is not only an extraordinary storyteller, but has psychic ability and an uncanny sense of timing. His fertile brain has dreamed up projects that have caused the U.S. government to wonder whether he was revealing secret plans and to question his timing when items in his strip appeared just as similar news stories were reported in the press.

While drawing *Terry,* Caniff in 1943 predicted a paratrooper invasion of Burma, which took place two weeks later. In 1949, *Steve Canyon* guessed the Russians were prefabricating submarines in their warmwater ports. It was revealed several months later that this was in fact happening. A number of similar incidents have occurred over the years in his strips.

Caniff has received numerous awards for his skillfully drawn stories and artwork. His originals have been displayed at leading art galleries around the world and segments of his work have been reprinted in the *Congressional Record.* His work is permanently preserved at Ohio State University, his alma mater.

But with all the praise and acclaim, Milton Caniff is disarmingly modest. His moon-like face (like his friend Bill Mauldin's) changes expression rapidly from intense concentration to a broad smile that spreads from one oversized ear to another. He is a walking encyclopedia, an animated speaker, and has the happy faculty of putting everyone at ease. He appears deeply interested in what is being said by the visitor. He really listens—a rare trait in the cartoon fraternity. Milton is relaxed and in charge of every situation.

Like most comic artists, Caniff, while proficient in lettering, has left this chore to an assistant. For years, Frank Engli, a competent cartoonist and creator of *Rocky the Stone Age Kid,* did the lettering honors. He recently died and another lexigrapher, Shel Dorf, has taken his place.

MISS LACE

Milton Caniff; *Miss Lace*—courtesy Camp Newspaper Service, U.S. Army

STEVE CANYON

Milton Caniff; *Steve Canyon*—reprinted with special permission of King Features Syndicate, Inc.

As a youngster I spent hours copying Caniff's characters: Terry, Pat, Connie, Big Stoop, and particularly the sensuous Dragon Lady and Burma. In a letter to Caniff I asked for an original drawing and enclosed a sketch of Terry, which I had laboriously lifted from the Sunday funnies. I water-colored the drawing and placed my request both in the note and in a balloon over Terry's head, hoping that the double whammy would do the trick.

Shortly thereafter, I received a note from Caniff complimenting me on the sketch and enclosing a color drawing of his own, personally inscribed. It was a lovely full-figure portrait of April Kane.

Actually, the drawing was a print, so skillfully reproduced that it looked like the real thing. Caniff or an assistant had "brushed over" some of the solid blacks to make it look as if it had been done by hand, and with the water-color overlay, it was very difficult to tell that the drawing was not an original.

I borrowed my dad's powerful magnifying glass, which he used to examine his stamp collection, in order to study April Kane up close. Even with the glass, it was difficult to determine the authenticity of the color drawing. After long study, I determined that Caniff had sent me a reproduction. So, another letter was directed to his home in New City, New York, requesting an original daily *Terry* strip. It was

Milton Caniff; reprinted from collection of Art Wood

"APRIL"
for ARTHUR & BILL WOOD,
WITH MY VERY BEST WISHES — Milton Caniff

some months before I had an answer, but one day a roll arrived in the mail with Caniff's distinctive handwriting. Enclosed was a beautiful original *Terry* daily, which is reproduced here. I was on Cloud Nine!

Of all the cartoonists, he has been the kindest and most helpful to those in the trade. He always has time for struggling artists, stu-dents, and those interested in cartooning. Perhaps this is because Billy Ireland, John T. McCutcheon, and many others gave him helpful advice when he was trying to decide whether to become an actor or an artist. His interest in people, however, is a deep and integral part of his warm and generous nature. Milton Caniff is, indeed, a genial genius.

STEVE CANYON

Milton Caniff; *Steve Canyon*—reprinted with special permission of King Features Syndicate, Inc.

22

Al Capp
FROM SEX TO SHMOO
AND BACK AGAIN

ALFRED G. CAPLIN, the creator of the famous comic strip *Li'l Abner,* was better known by his pseudonym Al Capp. His wonder-world of irascible hillbilly characters entertained millions of readers around the world, making Dogpatch more famous than London, Paris, Moscow, or even Lower Slobbovia. At the strip's peak it appeared in more than 900 newspapers. *Abner* was adapted into a Broadway hit, debuted in the movies, and provided Capp a vast audience on radio, television, and the lecture circuit. The burly cartoonist with a lame leg and nervous laugh was always friendly on the surface but rather distant and hard to get to know. Like Abner, Capp had a shock of unruly curly hair, a large bulbous nose, a protruding chin, and a dirty grin. Unlike Abner, he was razor-sharp in intellect and fast on the draw. Early in his career he had worked with fellow cartoonist Milton Caniff at the AP, and they were good chums. Milt introduced me to Capp at a National Cartoonists Society dinner in New York in the late 'forties. I saw him intermittently over the years, and although he was effusive, gracious, and always helpful, he was not a close friend. Capp had suffered a leg amputation as a youngster but overcame his disability, walking with a confident limp. He often spoke at hospitals and veterans centers to encourage the handicapped.

Despite early discouragements—physical and occupational—he became one of the most skillful writers and satirists in the business. Capp oozed talent—as a critic, commentator, comic artist, and speaker. He was acid and mercurial, unpredictable and irreverent, witty and biting. He was in fact an earthy Renaissance man—a blend of Dante, Rabelais, and Milton. John Steinbeck rated him one of America's best writers and worthy of a Nobel Prize. Steinbeck had this to say:

> I have met Al Capp a number of times, a stocky man who scowls at other men and melts disgustingly at women. I am sure that he is the best satirist since Laurence Sterne. He has taken our customs, our dreams, our habits of thought, our social structure, our economics, examined them gently like amusing bugs. Then he has pulled a nose a little longer, made outstanding ears a little more outstanding, described it in a dreadful folk poetry, and returned it to us in a hilarious picture of our ridiculous selves but with such good nature that we seem to have thought of it ourselves.
>
> Capp has invented names which have become completely accepted parts of our lives, such as Big Barnsmell, the outside man at the Skonk Works, Hairless Joe, and Robin Hoodlum, whose motto is, "I take from the rich and give to the poor, namely me."
>
> He makes savage forays into other fields but his favorite hunting ground is the American family. The hero, Li'l Abner, big, strong,

141

beautiful, innocent, and illiterate, the very archetype of the football player our daughters fall in love with every autumn. Daisy Mae, innocent, stupid, beautiful, constant, virginal, and naked, in a word every adolescent's dream girl. Li'l Abner's mother, small, tough, the best fighter in Dogpatch, the ruler of the family and the community, the real matriarch, and yet capable of going into a tight spin and passing a miracle. The father of the family, stupid, ineffectual, lovable, and bumbling. Only now and then does Pa emerge to dignity and effectiveness, under Yokum's Moon (surely one of the great conceptions) and when he becomes a gold sniffer after eating Presarved Tarnips. There is a fine crazy consistency about all of this that is terrifying. Dogpatch is a very real place to us.

As another commentator reflected, Capp drew his famous *Li'l Abner* strip on three levels: the basic story line, a critique of current society, and a mystical personal interpretation of life centered about his own set of homespun characters.

Capp had a tough time breaking into the

business. He shifted from one art school to another, a short step ahead of the bill collector. But he was persistent and loud. "My problem is that whatever I do is so noisy," he once commented. No one was going to shut up the controversial kid from Boston. He was determined to be a successful cartoonist, and neither privation nor poverty were to hinder his progress once he had his sights set on the top of the India ink bottle.

LI'L ABNER

Al Capp; *Li'l Abner*—©1987, Capp Enterprises, Inc. All rights reserved

Al started his cartoon career as an assistant to Ham Fisher, the creator of the comic *Joe Palooka*. Ham had spotted Al on the street with a portfolio of drawings and had hired him on the spot for a song. The relationship was a stormy and tempestuous one. Capp drew a sequence concerning a group of French hillbillies for the Fisher strip, and when he parted ways to start his own comic, *Li'l Abner*, for United Feature Syndicate, Ham Fisher claimed plagiarism. Fisher spent the rest of his life trying to prove that Capp had stolen his

LI'L ABNER

LI'L ABNER

idea, and to make matters worse, claimed that Capp was featuring thinly disguised pornography in *Li'l Abner*. Suits and countersuits followed until Ham Fisher died by his own hand in 1955.

It is true that Capp featured sexy sequences in his strip—with such showstoppers as the voluptuous Daisy Mae, dirty but darling Moonbeam McSwine, and the sensuous wolf girl. Thousands of fans looked forward to provocative continuity with an off-beat quality—and Capp did not disappoint his readers. The script was spicy and full of innuendoes. Even the syndicate executives went through Capp's advance proofs with a fine-toothed comb trying to determine if the material was X-rated or just suggestive. The cartoonist not only poked fun at sex but ridiculed everything, including himself, and frequently featured his own likeness in *Li'l Abner*.

Al Capp also varied the strip's diet with endearing animals, the shmoos, loveable little creatures who sacrificed themselves for the common good; Kigmies, who loved to be kicked around; and Abner's favorite pig companion, Salomey. These creations often challenged the popularity of the main characters.

Capp, like Caniff, used world-famous personalities in his comic strip, thinly disguised with outrageous names to hide their identity. Those pictured included Winston Churchill (Adorable Jones), George Bernard Shaw (Adam Lazonga), Jane Russell (Moonbeam McSwine), former New York Mayor Fiorello LaGuardia (Marryin' Sam), Veronica Lake (Daisy Mae), and countless others.

Early on, he was criticized by the conservatives for his liberal views. In later years, he was condemmed by the political left for his tirades against S.W.I.N.E. (Students Wildly

LI'L ABNER

LI'L ABNER

Al Capp; Li'l Abner—© 1987, Capp Enterprises, Inc. All rights reserved

Indignant About Nearly Everything) and the folk singers who formed the core of protest in the 'sixties. "When conservatives were fraudulent, I attacked them," Capp said. "The liberals loved me. The conservatives maintained an icy silence. Then liberalism became too suffocatingly smug. I attacked them. The conservatives continued to maintain an icy silence. But the liberals didn't. They rose from one end of the country to the other and denounced me. It was a shock to realize that graduates of Smith and clergymen knew language like that." He was sued by Joan Baez for his searing satire on folk singers who Capp said tried to cover anti-Americanism with a patriotic veneer. His political comments which had turned 180 degrees sent shivers up the spines of some who claimed Capp was a traitor.

Capp hit his stride in the late 'thirties and was his best in the early 'forties. As the years rolled by, his interest in the strip diminished, and the work was relegated to a group of talented ghosts who never mastered his savage touch. On his own initiative, the strip was discontinued in 1968. At the end of his life, Capp

suffered from fatigue, emphysema, and a general physical breakdown. After a long, hard fight, he died in his suburban Boston home on November 5, 1979.

Capp's work is classic and will long be remembered by historians for the creation of Sadie Hawkins Day, the continuing battle of wits between Abner and Daisy, and the political tomfoolery of Senator Jack S. Phogbound and General Jubilation T. Cornpone. He left a legacy of fun and foolishness unequalled in the annals of American humor.

23

Fitzpatrick
AMERICAN DAUMIER

FROM THE late 'thirties to the 'fifties, the king of American political cartoonists was Daniel R. Fitzpatrick of the *St. Louis Post-Dispatch*. He ruled supreme. Influenced by Honore Daumier and his immediate predecessor, Robert Minor, he drew in broad crayon strokes with assurance and power. While simple in construction, his cartoons were dramatic and hard-hitting and covered every subject from corruption in St. Louis to the Nazi menace. His swastika-marked tanks crushing the people of Europe became a symbol of the German war machine.

Fitz was as tough as his cartoons. Tall, Prussian, and curt, he was both admired and feared by his fellow artists. He was good, and he knew it. He won two Pulitzer Prizes—one in 1926 and another in 1955. He was awarded an honorary degree from Washington University in St. Louis and a citation from the University of Missouri for his "distinguished service to journalism."

My father visited Fitz in his office in St. Louis in the early 'forties to request an original drawing for my collection. Fitz threw him out.

Bruce Russell, Pulitzer Prize-winning cartoonist of the *Los Angeles Times,* entertained Fitzpatrick during a visit to the West Coast in 1946. This was the year that Russell had won the Pulitzer. After drinks and dinner, Bruce also requested a Fitz original to hang in his

office. Without batting an eye, Fitz replied, "I'll be glad to send you one, Bruce, but it will cost you a hundred and fifty dollars." Russell declined the offer.

The first year the American Association of Cartoonists was formed, Fitzpatrick traveled to Washington to attend the meeting. I was young in the business, but called him and invited him to lunch. To my surprise, he accepted, and we met in the dining room of the Statler-Hilton Hotel. His bark turned out to be worse than his bite. He was a delight, and I enjoyed his company. Of course, I was new in the trade and certainly offered no competition. With competitors, his behavior was very different.

Tom Little of the *Nashville Tennessean* was a cartoonist who drew in much the same style as Fitzpatrick, and Fitzpatrick resented it. Tom, whose size matched his name, was also in attendance at that first organizational meeting of the political cartoonists' society. It had just been announced that Little had won the Pulitzer Prize. Tom Little had never met Fitzpatrick and was anxious to visit with the man he had so long admired.

After the banquet, a long line of cartoonists queued up to shake hands with the great cartoonist of Pulitzer's paper. Diminutive Tom was at the very end. As his turn came, he stuck out his hand and said, "Mr. Fitzpatrick, my

IN THE "ANYTHING MAY HAPPEN" STAGE.

name is Tom Little and I have long admired . . ." Before another word could be spoken, Fitz turned brusquely away, saying, "I never cared for imitators." Tom Little went back to his room and wept.

Despite Fitzpatrick's abrasive side, his relationship with me was a long and pleasant one. I had favorably reviewed his book *Cartoons by Fitzpatrick,* and the review had been reprinted widely around the country. In it I said:

> Fitzpatrick's powerful style, familiar to newspaper readers throughout the world, has been acclaimed by the modern art world and often compared to that of Daumier and Goya. His ability to depict the complex in simple terms has placed him among the top three or four cartoonists of our generation.
>
> . . . This first major collection of Fitzpatrick's work pulls no punches. It is a graphic picture of the great depression, the world war and the cold war of today. This is a record of a generation drawn and told by a man who in the words of Joseph Pulitzer "ranks at or near the head of that great procession of men who have drawn pictures with a purpose, the purpose being to make things at least a little better in this great country and in this distraught world."

Fitzpatrick wrote a gracious note thanking me for the kind words. He also sent me an original autographed cartoon—gratis. We corresponded until his retirement in 1958. After his retirement, Fitzpatrick produced sixteen half-hour television programs for Educational Television depicting his work habits. He traveled and continued to paint until his death in 1969.

Tom Little; reprinted by permission,
The Tennessean, Nashville, TN; a Gannett Newspaper

24

Cyrus Cotton Hungerford

Hungerford

IN 1956 I joined the staff of the *Pittsburgh Press* as chief editorial cartoonist. The *Press* had one of the largest art staffs in America, and I was fortunate to work with this distinguished group. I soon came to know and admire the noted cartoonist of the opposition newspaper, the *Pittsburgh Post-Gazette*. His charismatic manner and innate kindness were quickly evident.

A few weeks after I arrived on the scene, a prestigious black-tie press dinner was held at the Pittsburgh Press Club. All the notables in the state were invited, including the staff of the three large dailies publishing in the Steel City. I knew few Pittsburghers, other than those in the editorial department of my own paper. I had been introduced to the legendary Cy Hungerford, but it was perfunctory and brief.

Photographers from all over Pennsylvania were busy taking the celebrities' pictures, and Cy's in particular. He was surrounded by a group of well-wishers and politicians.

"Hold it, Cy, stand closer to the governor," one photographer demanded.

I stood in the back of the room, lonely and uncomfortable, watching the activity. Cy spotted me, and I saw him whisper in the ear of a *Post-Gazette* photographer. A few minutes later I was surrounded by photographers who asked if they could get a photograph of the new cartoonist in town. This kindness was so typical of the city's best-loved citizen.

To Pittsburghers, gentle, genial, gregarious, bald-headed cartoonist Cyrus Cotton Hungerford was more famous in the state than William Penn, and his reputation reached into the far corners of the earth. Dean of American editorial cartoonists, Hungerford worked until he was ninety-four, and was a national figure in his field, recognized in other lands as one of the most famous of all American cartoonists. Few artists can claim his achievements or longevity. He retired in late August of 1977 after sixty-five years as cartoonist for the *Pittsburgh Post-Gazette* and its predecessor, the *Pittsburgh Sun*, which he joined in 1912. This was truly a record in American journalism.

Hungerford's cartoon career dated back even further, to his teens, when he drew editorial cartoons for the *Parkersburg (West Virginia) Sentinel*, the *Dispatch-News*, and the *Social Rebel*, making his drawings on chalk plates with a stylus. Cy started as a cartoonist at the tender age of thirteen—unlucky for some but lucky for the ambitious and talented youth who worked for the local papers after school. His cartoons drew immediate attention and a lawsuit. In one, he depicted a man with one hand robbing a bank and the other choking

Cyrus Cotton "Cy" Hungerford; reprinted by permission: Pittsburgh *Post-Gazette*

FIDEL'S LATEST GREETING

Always active and imaginative, Cy started drawing a comic strip after World War I. *Snoodles,* a mischievous "Dennis the Menace"-like character, was syndicated by the George Matthew Adams Service and appeared in newspapers throughout the country from 1914 to 1928, when he tired of the six-comics-a-week stint in addition to his regular editorial cartoons. *Snoodles* was a special favorite of the noted *Chicago Tribune* cartoonist and fellow Hoosier, John T. McCutcheon. Cy also contributed to a Comic Art Series in which he put down helpful tips to those interested in this branch of the profession. Here are a few sample quotes from his correspondence course in 1916:

> Humor, especially good clean humor, is the backbone that holds a comic together and makes it live. The old "slapstick-knock-down-and-drag-out" style of humor is still much in vogue with cartoonists but an overdose of it grows monotonous to the news-

widows and orphans, and he recently reminisced, "I put his name right on it, too." Cy always told it like it was, and luckily for him, a kind local district attorney rescued the youngster from the clutches of the grand jury.

Cy quickly refined the difficult technique of drawing on chalk plates—first sketching the cartoon on thin paper, then tracing it in reverse, and finally etching the plate, blowing the dust away during the process—a messy and intricate job permitting no mistakes, for a false stroke could not be erased. Cy not only did the drawing but also his own casting, pouring hot metal onto the plates in a casting box. Frequently he burned his fingers, which accounted for his affinity for a cool glass filled with ice cubes and Old Granddad.

From Parkersburg, Hungerford moved on to the *Wheeling Register* where he doubled as cartoonist and reporter. He remained in Wheeling for four years before heading for the Steel City and a job with the *Pittsburgh Sun.*

A CARTOONIST'S GREAT LOSS

Cyrus Cotton "Cy" Hungerford; reprinted by permission: Pittsburgh *Post-Gazette*

SOME WEATHER

paper reader and the future comic artist must try to inject more real wit and less brickbats into his drawings. The average reader laughs louder at a clever plot worked out consistently than he does at a comic filled with a conglomeration of animated figures that have little or no significance. Of course a point can be driven home by showing a fellow tapping another on his soft head with a hard brick. In real life this would mean the calling of policemen and patrol wagons but comic paper people seem to have license to assault and batter without even being reprimanded.

The *idea* is the nest egg from which any clever comic is hatched. Without the foundation of a funny idea to build a comic strip upon, the whole business crumbles away and falls very flat indeed. When a reader glances over a comic he expects to find a bright, original surprise in it somewhere. If he fails to discover that little laugh-provoking surprise he immediately loses interest and lays it aside with the remark, "Punk! Nothing to it." An idea is an elusive germ. It is the one thing that cannot be taught the embryo cartoonist. Your imagination must furnish ideas. Train your imagination to search for them. Look about you and develop the habit of exaggerating any amusing incident that you see or hear of in every day life.

Timely topics of the day furnish good material for strip ideas. A comic touching on some current event that is being talked about is always appreciated by the public. One cause for the great success of *Mutt and Jeff* is the fact that they keep abreast with the times. If they are not recruiting in European armies they are crossing the Mexican border to fight Villa.

Cy also did his part during the second World War when, again moving in new directions, he developed a series of defense posters "designed to rouse peaceful citizens to deeds of daring and hard work." These posters were featured in defense factories, urging workers "to obey regulations, work hard, keep their mouths shut, and look out for fifth columnists and saboteurs." Hungerford and advertising friend George Sherman traveled to Washington to consult with FBI Director J. Edgar Hoover who endorsed the series, giving encouragement and ideas. The drawings, an overnight success, were plastered on the walls of plants and factories from coast to coast. *Life*

magazine devoted three full pages in its "Speaking of Pictures" section to the innovative posters backing the war effort.

One of Cy's cartoon characters featured Pa Pitt, a plump colonial wearing a periwig, breeches, and hose. Pa Pitt was a bemused, sometimes baffled, observer of the modern scene. In a way Cy was like him. Too down-to-earth to be Olympian, he laughed at life and life laughed with him.

Cy Hungerford, with friend and publisher Paul Block, Jr., toured the world covering major news events. His assignments took him to Europe, North Africa, Mexico, the West Indies, and South America. He covered the coronation of King George VI in 1937, the wedding of the Duke of Windsor that same year, and the wedding and coronation of Queen Elizabeth in 1947 and 1953. He was one of the first to do an on-the-spot series of life in England, France, Greece, and Italy after World War II. Cy did special cross-page cartoons of his travels, mailing the drawings back to the *Post-Gazette* which featured them prominently. In Rome, Cy had a private audience with Pope Pius XII. When the pope asked Cy if he might give a blessing to his children, Cy, who was childless, said no, but that he would appreciate a good word for his terrier Jiggs, who had a bad habit of biting everyone. The pope, who loved dogs himself, shared a laugh with the forthright Pittsburgh cartoonist.

Bill Block, the publisher of the *Pittsburgh Post-Gazette* and a long-time Hungerford admirer, over the years had given Cy a free hand on the editorial page. That is why his cartoons always had a fresh and free quality. Cy gave up the pen-and-ink technique of his early chalk plate days for the broader strokes of a brush, and his distinctive style was as forthright as his political opinion. His drawings were full of vitality and motion, rendered in a quick but studied fashion. His caricatures captured in a few strokes the personality of his subjects, always with good humor.

While other cartoonists portrayed their victims in intricate cross-hatch style, filling the faces with a sea of lines, Cy's caricatures were done in bare-brush outline, but always capturing the likeness. His original cartoons

COAL STRIKE EYEBROWS

were in much demand by local and national politicians.

Cy Hungerford's cartoons have been widely reprinted over the years. He was a regular in the old *Cartoons Magazine* which selected the best work of the nation's cartoonists.

Hungerford's work spanned the administrations of fourteen presidents, most of whom he knew personally. The originals of his cartoons,

which for many years appeared on the front page of the paper, were requested by presidents and prime ministers alike. His work has decorated the executive offices of the White House and the walls of numerous Congressmen and Cabinet members.

In more recent years, his work appeared in the *New York Times'* "News of the Week in Review" section, *Time* magazine, *U.S. News* and *World Report, Newsweek*—in fact, most of the national journals. He won the National Headliners Award in 1945 and was honored by two national honorary fraternities, Sigma Delta Chi and Omicron Delta Kappa. He was also given a degree of Doctor of Arts by Washington and Jefferson College. The Association of American Editorial Cartoonists gave him a special citation at its convention in Washington where he visited with President Ford at the White House. At a Hungerford award dinner in Pittsburgh, one of many, at the Penn Sheraton Hotel in 1957, the distinguished historian Charles F. Lewis had this to say:

> Cy Hungerford is an eclectic. Universal in his interests, he reaches out into manifold fields of human activity, with rare gifts of understanding and analysis, selects that which is important and good, and takes it to himself. Then comes the process of synthesis, a piece of cardboard, a pen and a little ink, and—behold—a cartoon.
>
> He does not crucify people. He laughs with them, not at them. But to the masks behind which some seek to hide, to the cloak of the hypocrite, to the talk of the double talker, he shows no mercy. As frequently, and perhaps more importantly, his drawing board glows with a warm, strong light that is directed upon examples of nobility, of courage, of sacrifice, and of unselfishness in achievement, qualities which, thank God, still are dominant in our country and in our city, in these troubled and uncertain times.

Cy Hungerford died in 1983 a short time before his 100th birthday. No one could be certain of his actual age, as he kept this fact and his drawing brush close to his vest.

Cyrus Cotton "Cy" Hungerford; reprinted by permission: Pittsburgh *Post Gazette*

TOO MUCH WATER FOR PA

25
Moco the Great

Yardley

As IS OFTEN the case in winter months, Washington D.C. was frozen into a lake of ice. The unreliable weatherman had predicted further precipitation. Despite the weather, the founding father of the Association of American Editorial Cartoonists, John Stampone, and I had planned a trip to Baltimore to see Richard Q. Yardley, the legendary Maryland cartoonist.

Yardley's nickname was "Moco," as well known in Baltimore as that of H. L. Mencken. For years Yardley had decorated the editorial pages of the *Baltimore Sun* in his distinct Oriental style. His homey cartoons on local politicians, seafood, and parodies of famous Baltimore hangouts were known throughout the state, and indeed the country. His drawings were rendered in a squiggly line and appeared regularly in the *Sun* and were reprinted in the "News of the Week" section of the *New York Times*. He drew in various shapes and sizes, depending on the subject matter, which could run five columns wide or six columns up and down the page.

Yardley often caricatured himself in his cartoons—a round, moon-like face with a drooping pancake beret covering a field of freckles. His cartoons also frequently featured a scrawny cat—a trademark as familiar to the eastern shore of Maryland as Felix or Krazy Kat.

The famous Baltimore cartoonist had served in the 175th Division during World War I, and often worked a military theme into his cartoons. Perhaps it was the ornate uniforms that appealed to his artistic eye; but whatever the reason, he delighted in picturing servicemen, whether the dogface in the trenches or such noted generals as Bradley and Eisenhower. He had a special fondness for a certain captain who served in the infantry as well as in the White House—Harry Truman. Often his Truman cartoons used World War I themes updated in the inimitable Yardley style. A famous cartoon showed Truman boiling mad over *Washington Post* critic Paul Hume's assessment of daughter Margaret Truman's voice. In the background of the drawing, China and Russia looked on in amazement from their vantage points across the world.

Yardley was a master at capturing uniforms and costumes—simplifying the designs but always retaining the flavor and vitality of the period depicted. His twirling suns and concentric designs were much in the tradition of Van Gogh.

Yardley was a character! He had invited me to lunch at the National Press Club the first year the political cartoonists met in 1957. As we walked through the lobby of the hotel enroute to the cabstand, we were accosted by

DISADVANTAGES OF BEING A
POLITICAL CARTOONIST

Foxo Reardon, the creator of the comic strip *Bozo,* who lived in Richmond, Virginia. Foxo had a severe drinking problem and, unlike Moco, could not handle his liquor. Although it was barely lunch-time, he was weaving bleary-eyed through the lobby. With signs and gestures he made it clear that he wanted to join us for lunch. Without batting an eye, Moco said, "Foxo, you go out and hail a cab. I've got to pick up a *Baltimore Sun* and we'll join you." Foxo, with great effort, wobbled toward the revolving door on K Street.

Yardley grabbed a paper and propelled me through the side door into a cab. When we got back an hour or so later from the Press Club, Foxo was still tottering precariously through the lobby. With great aplomb and mock indignation, Moco went up to him. "Foxo, where have you been? You've treated us

shamelessly! Art and I waited over an hour outside and you never showed up!" Foxo was all apologies.

Stampone and I knew that Moco had suffered a series of strokes that had made drawing difficult, if not impossible. In addition, he had cataracts on both eyes and, despite successive operations, was immobile. Yardley had consequently retired from the newspaper in 1969 to become a passive political observer. He had been hospitalized and thereafter convalesced in a nursing home overlooking his beloved Baltimore Harbor. He was now back home again. Stampone and I called ahead to make sure he was up to seeing us and headed to Baltimore.

His comfortable home in the suburbs was draped with icicles. The throughways were covered with snow except for thin tire tracks

Richard Q. Yardley; reprinted by permission: Baltimore *Sun*

EUROPEAN MILITARY COSTUMES, ONCE SO COLORFUL AND DISTINCTIVE •••

down the middle of the street. We skidded to a stop outside his house, parked in a snow bank, and hoped to be able to extricate ourselves.

Moco was seated in a large lounge chair smoking a cigarette when we entered. His white hair was askew, making him look even more the artist. He had acquired a mustache, and his wife informed us that he had shaved his beard especially for our visit. A seldom-used walker was propped at the side of his chair, and he was intently reading a copy of *The New Yorker.*

He seemed to recognize us and greeted us warmly but continued to read the magazine, glancing up from time to time to acknowledge a remark or make a comment.

Yardley was not a gregarious person, but he had a keen mind and a highly developed sense of Irish humor. His memory was shaken by his series of strokes, and he had difficulty recalling details and names. He remembered clearly past events and trips, however, particularly one to England which he had made with a group of cartoonists in 1973. Yardley loved England with its pomp and circumstance. He was awed by Westminister Abbey and took careful note of the carved sarcophagi, tapestries, and hanging banners. He also relished Stratford-upon-Avon, and commented that he had never been happier than sitting on a hill overlooking the church where Shakespeare was buried, sipping ale. We chatted about the trip and recalled a number of incidents that

seemed to stimulate his interest, but he continued to stare at *The New Yorker,* paging through the magazine over and over again. Moco's talented and lovely wife, Peggy, herself an artist of note, sat with us as we reminisced and tears welled in her eyes.

Yardley, of course, could not go upstairs. The dining room had been converted into a bedroom complete with hospital bed. The walls, however, were gaily decorated with his own beautifully designed and colorful maps of Maryland, peppered with tiny cartoon characters.

We were anxious to obtain several of Moco's original drawings, so Peggy invited us to the cellar where a large cupboard was packed with his old cartoons. The basement was raw, cold, and dusty. We shuffled hurriedly through the panels and political cartoons neatly piled together, rubbing our hands to keep warm. Out of earshot, Mrs. Yardley told us that Moco had given up. "He refuses to draw anymore," she said sadly. "He can, but he won't, and it breaks my heart." When we went back upstairs, I hesitated to ask him to sign the drawings for fear that it would be too great an effort. He made no move to autograph the cartoons.

Despite his affliction, Yardley still relished a bourbon-on-the-rocks. "Peggy, bring the boys a drink," he said, "and while you are at it, bring me one, too." It was the same old Yardley. He could drink more and show it less than any artist in the business.

26

Presidents Are Human, Too!

PRESIDENTS of the United States have been known to crumble with fatigue, look ghastly on television, feel queasy, lose their voices, and forget names like anyone else. They must, however, foster an image of perfection that is projected to the public by the White House staffers and advance men. When the chief executive stumbles or hits his head climbing into a plane or boat, like other travelers frequently do, it becomes a major news event—a national happening. Such is the penalty of prominence.

I cannot claim to be a close friend of presidents, but as a cartoonist I have observed nine presidents close up—blemishes and all. I have studied their expressions, movements, gestures, and posture in order to better render them in my cartoons. Roosevelt was known for his huge chin, Truman for his military walk, Eisenhower for his grin, Kennedy for his wavy hair, Johnson for his drawl and big ears, and Nixon for his ski-nose and "making things perfectly clear" with upraised arms and "V-for-Victory" symbol. Jerry Ford was famous for his protruding jaw, and Jimmy Carter for his mouth full of teeth—unmatched since the days of Teddy Roosevelt—and Reagan for his wavy hair and wrinkles. But other traits and characteristics were also important to define character. For instance, Kennedy had a habit of poking his finger straight at the audience like the Uncle Sam in James Montgomery Flagg's famous war poster, "I Want You."

It takes a while to capture the likeness of a president in caricature. That is why a president looks more and more like his cartoon likeness as his term progresses.

The first time I saw President Kennedy was during the 1960 presidential campaign in Pittsburgh. He was on a lengthy speaking tour and was exhausted. I had heard how young he looked, but close up he looked like an old man—baggy, sunken eyes, and lines of fatigue crossing his face. His suit was rumpled, and he was whipped.

His brother, Bobby, had come to Pittsburgh early as an advance man and had run into a buzz saw, as Pennsylvania Gov. David Lawrence, one of the last big-city bosses and a Catholic himself, had presidential aspirations of his own. There were reports of fireworks and hard feelings. The presidential candidate was late as he had been all during the campaign. He had two speeches to give in Pittsburgh—one at the Mosque, Pittsburgh's indoor stadium, and one in the Hill District, the city's black community.

Accompanying the candidate was a host of aides, including Larry O'Brien and Adam Clayton Powell, the Baptist minister and congressman from New York. I sat next to Powell at lunch and was astounded to see him stash away a couple of double martinis as if he were downing a tumbler of water. He was an animated conversationalist and was on hand to warm up the crowd in the black section of Pittsburgh.

I had done some advance work, too. Early on the morning of the Kennedy appearance, I had met with Pierre Salinger, his press assistant, at the Hilton Hotel across from the newspaper, overlooking Pittsburgh's historic Point Park. The meeting had a two-fold purpose for me— to get to know Pierre and to make arrangements to walk out with the candidate after the Mosque appearance in order to have one of my cartoons autographed by Kennedy. I had drawn a cartoon depicting the Democratic donkey with a Kennedy hairdo and was anxious to have the candidate sign the original for a collection of my cartoons autographed by presidents. The cartoon I had done that day for the *Press,* however, was unfavorable to the candidate. The *Pittsburgh Press* was not supporting Kennedy, as the paper had close ties to Governor Lawrence. My *Press* cartoon depicted Kennedy backing a car off a cliff while standing up in the front and mouthing his campaign motto, "Let's move America forward." It was bad timing to say the least.

HOW'S THAT AGAIN?

Art Wood; courtesy Pittsburgh *Press*

The Mosque where Kennedy was to speak was crowded, and, despite his fatigue, the candidate came to life with the bright lights and applause. I was seated right below the podium with a number of my *Press* colleagues. Shirley Uhl, political reporter for the *Press,* feature writer Sam Hood, and I had press and police clearance to meet Kennedy immediately following his talk to walk with him to the limousine where I planned to ask about the cartoon.

When the speech ended, the three of us moved to the roped-off area, as did Mayor and Mrs. Joseph Barr. We spoke briefly to the candidate and, with the police holding hands to ward off the crowd, tried to get out of the auditorium. Then an unexpected event took place. The girls along the exit route leaped over the police lines and grabbed Kennedy by his tie, ripping off his cuff links and pulling his handkerchief from his coat pocket. He tried to smile and be gracious, but the scene approached riot stages. Mrs. Barr was slugged in the jaw as one of the teenagers grabbed for Kennedy. She was dazed by the blow and was being held up by a police officer as the already red-faced mayor tried to stem the tide. It was a useless effort.

Reporter Shirley Uhl slipped and fell. The girls walked right over him, vying for position. He suffered a fractured elbow. Fortunately, I managed to get ahead of Kennedy as the crush of the crowd accelerated the movement forward. The police grouped together and with the Secret Service helped cordon off the screaming women. It was an unbelievable sight.

The hapless candidate rushed for the car. I had a few words with him and hastily produced the cartoon I hoped to have signed. "When you do a *favorable* cartoon, Art, I'll sign it," he grinned, and disappeared into the limousine.

My friend Sam Hood laughed out loud. "Better luck next president," he said. Sam grapped my arm and directed me to a police car near the curb. "Come on," he said, "we'll give you a lift back to the paper." So I climbed into the patrol car for a ride to the *Press.*

"Art, I've got to stop and pick up a package at Kaufmann's Department Store," Sam said. "Come on with me and we'll walk back to the shop." I was facing a tight deadline, so I declined and said I'd ride back to the paper with the officer. So the police car stopped to let Sam out. It was the last time I ever saw my old friend.

A few minutes later, as he was about to enter the department store, a city bus with faulty brakes careened onto the sidewalk, pinning Sam to the side of the building. Two other passersby also were killed. I had missed death by a hair.

Because of the similarity of our names, Hood and Wood, and because we had been seen together, it was reported over the radio that we had both been killed. My wife heard news commentator Bill Burns make the announcement. Not knowing what had transpired, I called home to check on a dinner date. My wife fainted. It had been a long and very sad day.

While we were in Pittsburgh, my youngest son Baldwin Jennings (Win) was born. His first spoken word was "car-toon."

The next time I saw Jack Kennedy, he was being addressed as "Mr. President," and was comfortably ensconced in the White House. It was a different and more pleasant occasion. We were there to present him with a collection of original cartoons especially drawn for the chief executive by the nation's political cartoonists. Members of the AAEC felt the president of the United States, so often caricatured, might like to see himself as the country's cartoonists pictured him, so in the early days of the Kennedy Administration special drawings of JFK were compiled in book form for presentation to the president. The book was bound in dark red leather with "President John F. Kennedy—as seen by the Association of American Editorial Cartoonists" stamped on the cover in gold type. Each cartoonist's name was set in type beneath his drawing with his paper listed under the name.

Kennedy was very much at ease and seemed unhurried and in fine humor. Scott Long, President of the AAEC, presented the album to

President Kennedy shows his book of caricatures to visiting cartoonists (from left) John Stampone, Jim Berryman, and Scott Long.

Kennedy, saying that he knew the president received many gifts, but that this was an unusual one. The president interrupted with a laugh to say that, on the contrary, he didn't receive a lot of presents at all, that Jackie got most of them, and that he was always glad to get one of his own. He then read Scott's letter aloud and laughed at the paragraph stating, "You will find here caricatures by men who have been opponents of both your policy and party." He looked my way and winked.

Kennedy graciously leafed through the book seeking out the drawings of the men present and looking at each one. He then paged through the volume, inspecting all the drawings. "Do you find that I am harder to draw than Ike?" Kennedy asked. Jim Berryman of the *Washington Star* replied that he found him easier to draw than Ike, and Scott said he found him harder to draw. We spent twenty-five minutes with the president and had held up a cabinet meeting.

It was some time, however, before I was to receive a Kennedy autograph on one of my original cartoons. While working for Scripps-Howard in Washington as a fill-in for cartoonist Talburt during his vacation, I did a cartoon on the subject of Bobby Kennedy's appointment as attorney general. It was a controversial appointment, and I submitted several roughs before getting an okay. The finished cartoon showed President Kennedy at his desk with a cabinet close by. Bob Kennedy's name was spelled out, B-O-B, with the O as a knob to a cabinet drawer labeled "Attorney General." And the title of the cartoon was, "Right Where He Can Reach It." This cartoon apparently fitted the "favorable" appellation, and the president signed it with a personal inscription. Later Sen. Robert Kennedy also signed the drawing.

At a later date President Kennedy invited the cartoonists to the White House for a reception in the Rose Garden. A display of original cartoons was arranged on the portico and the president kidded us about his "jowls" and the "unfair" treatment he was receiving at the hands of the group. He seemed to relish the contact and mixed freely with the cartoonists, visiting with old friends and making new ones. The cartoonists sketched him as he wandered about, and he peered over their shoulders as they drew him, fascinated with the various renditions, some complimentary, some fearful. He laughed at them all.

In 1956 I left the *Pittsburgh Press* to give television a try. With the idea that television cartooning was an untapped field, I produced a series of short cartoon commentaries, which I did "live" on tape. I actually drew a political cartoon on camera and while drawing commented on the particular story in the news. It seemed to me a great idea, as the public has always enjoyed watching an artist at work. I invested my own money, had television friends in Pittsburgh tape the sequences, and headed to New York for fame and fortune. The show received mixed reviews. Some thought it had great potential. Others felt it was a distraction to draw and talk at the same time. I spent over a year and a great deal of money trying to sell the concept. The idea was brought down by the "equal time" ruling. At that time television was hesitant to really get rough and felt if a strong view was expressed in one direction, an equally strong view would have to be shown on the other side of the issue. Two cartoonists

doing different cartoons diametrically opposed in the same time slot didn't make sense—economically or otherwise—the executives concluded. I still think it is a good idea.

At any rate, with a lot of money down the drain and no income, I had to get a job. I wanted to be in my hometown of Washington, D.C. The cartoon bases were filled and through friends, I made contact with a national association looking for someone with a journalistic background to work on a Washington newsletter. So I joined the U.S. Independent Telephone Association (the 2,000-plus non-Bell telephone companies) where I edited the association's publications and served as a cartoonist for its various journals. From doing seven or eight cartoons each week, I slipped into a comfortable schedule of two or three—more in the tradition of the British cartoonists.

During this period President Kennedy had been assassinated and Lyndon Johnson was sworn in as president. Johnson had been a speaker at the Washington meeting of cartoonists when we had been guests of Kennedy at the White House. My Dad, a long-time staunch Democrat, had known Johnson politically. He also was acquainted with the Carpenters, Les and Liz, a Washington journalistic team who represented a string of Texas newspapers and who were very close to the Johnson family. They had both been kind to me as a youngster getting started in the business.

I had done a caricature of Johnson for one of my television segments and went to Les and Liz in the hope of adding another autographed caricature to my wall of presidents. It was not a flattering cartoon of Johnson, but I thought it was a good likeness. Liz had taken a sabbatical and a job at the White House as LBJ's right-hand aide, and I asked if she could, in an off moment, talk to President Johnson on my behalf. Graciously she agreed.

However, months went by with no word. I called Les and he said the president had not been able to get to it. A few weeks later I ran into him at the Press Club. "Any news on the cartoon, Les?" I inquired. Sheepishly, Les took me aside and said, "Let me tell you what really happened. We didn't know how to tell you. Liz

President Lyndon B. Johnson with his telephone and caricatures.

took the cartoon into LBJ and he fumed, 'It's lousy! I won't sign the son-of-a-bitch.' " This news just made me more determined than ever to get a drawing autographed by Johnson.

President Johnson collected originals and was a cartoon enthusiast, leaving the job of contacting the nation's cartoonists for original drawings to a lovely lady, a relative of Mrs. Johnson, Willie Day Taylor. Willie Day was knowledgeable and, with her Southern charm, was most persuasive with the nation's cartoonists. She was close to the president, both by blood and location, as her quarters were near the Oval Office, and she had ready access to him. All of us were glad that Willie Day was there.

Through her good efforts a meeting with LBJ was arranged to present him a book of cartoons. John Milt Morris of the AP was president of the AAEC at the time, and we carefully worked out a scenario. I hoped to get a drawing autographed and suggested a plan to John. We would all have blowups made of the caricature each of those present had made of the president. This could be logically explained as an aid to the photographers. Then

the minute the president called in the press, John would lean over and ask that the president sign the cartoons for the few of us present. With the press covering the event, I felt it would be hard for Johnson to say no, and it worked just as we had planned. LBJ reluctantly signed the caricature I had done of him, as well as those of the others.

In the press of the crowd and with photographers pushing everywhere, I accidentally knocked the red telephone—one of the three phones the president had on his desk—to the floor. It made a loud dinging noise, and Johnson's face flushed as he glared at me with his cold, slate-blue eyes. "Excuse me, Mr. President," I said as I placed the telephone back on his desk. He didn't say a word, but his face was crimson and I felt the tension.

One of the press photographers did not make out as well. He had flipped the ashes from his cigarette on the carpet of the Oval Office. LBJ exploded. "What in the hell do you think you are doing?" he exclaimed. "Would you dump ashes on your carpet at home?" "Well, er . . . no . . . ," the photographer stammered. "Well, dammit, don't do it here!" the president shouted. "If you don't have respect for me at least have some respect for the office." The photographer made a hasty retreat, and so did we.

Lyndon Johnson, however, was good to the cartoonists. In a televised talk from the East Room he later said: "I know that I am talking to the most influential journalists in America. Reporters may write and politicians may talk, but what you draw remains in the public memory long after these other words are forgotten."

He also invited the cartoonists to the LBJ Ranch for a day. It was a most informal time, with us sitting around the pool and chatting as if we were all part of the family. Lynda Bird and her girls were there, as well as Lady Bird, who charmed everyone. Johnson personally greeted each man as the cartoonists filed into the ranch house on the Pedernales. There were soft drinks and *hors d'oeuvres,* and it was like an old-fashioned country picnic, sitting on deck chairs and making small talk.

After the social, Lyndon wanted to take us on a tour of his place, and it was *some* tour. After my faux pas at the White House, I thought I was *persona non grata.* But when President Johnson reached the point of the tour where his playhouse was located, he suddenly grabbed me by the arm and propelled me indoors to an old-fashioned grind telephone hanging on the wall. "See that phone, Art? That's the phone I used as a kid when we didn't have all those fancy numbers, just five digits and an operator that knew everyone. Those were the days!" Knowing that Johnson loved telephones, I was interested in what he had to say. "Did you know, Art, that my first job was with an independent telephone company? One of your outfits. My Uncle Baines had a small telephone company and I used to string wire and work for him." My colleagues were astounded with this unusual bit of information. "And these are my toys, the ones I played with," he volunteered, pointing out a drum and other assorted games and toys.

After a tour of the ranch, President Johnson took us to the LBJ Theatre. A slide presentation, over which the president presided, was

beautifully put together, but for some reason the picture overlapped the screen and the edges reflected off the wall. To me it was distracting. When I returned home I wrote LBJ a note pointing this out. I received a personal reply saying that he agreed and that the problem was being corrected. LBJ was a man for detail.

Of all the political leaders I have encountered, Richard Nixon was the most difficult to assess. I first met him in 1957 when his friend and occasional bridge partner, Jim Berryman, was suddenly taken ill. Jim called Sallie and me to pinch-hit as hosts for the Nixons during a cartoonist's cocktail party at the Press Club. Nixon was then vice-president under Eisenhower.

Nixon was easy to entertain, and I found him affable and attractive. Mrs. Nixon was also gracious and down-to-earth, and I was happy with the assignment. Nixon worked best in small groups, where he appeared relaxed and comfortable, in marked contrast to the wooden

President Richard Nixon chats with cartoonists beside his personal cartoon collection in the Executive Office Building.

White House photo

image he projected on television or at political rallies.

Sponsored by Berryman and others, Nixon was made an honorary member of the AAEC in 1957. Daniel Fitzpatrick, political cartoonist for the *St. Louis Post-Dispatch,* immediately resigned from the association. Nixon took his membership in AAEC seriously and traveled to Kansas City to attend the cartoonists' convention at the Muehlebach Hotel.

President Nixon did not regularly use the Oval Office, but preferred an office at the Executive Office Building, reserving the Oval Office for state occasions. His anteroom at the EOB was plastered with cartoons, most of them done by California cartoonists Bruce Russell, Newton Pratt, and Lou Grant. When a group of us arrived at the White House, early for the presentation of specially-drawn caricatures we were escorted into the outer reception room to wait. Who would have thought the place was bugged! I often wondered what we might have said that afternoon while waiting around for Ron Zeigler, Herb Klein, and the president.

When Nixon arrived, he was jaunty and self-assured, giving each of us souvenir golf balls embellished with his name as he related anecdotes about his cartoon collection. He took us into the inner office, which was lined with cases filled with gifts from foreign potentates and his extensive elephant collection. The president's elephants were encrusted with gems and semi-precious stones.

I'd brought with me two cartoons I hoped to have autographed—a large caricature of Nixon and the original of a cartoon I had done for the *Pittsburgh Press* during Nixon's unsuccessful campaign for governor of California. My wife pleaded with me not to take along the *Press* cartoon as she thought the president would be offended. It was a very unflattering drawing of Nixon as an elephant with his ski-nose as a trunk. The president autographed the large caricature and asked what was in the brown envelope.

"Well, Mr. President," I replied, "my wife told me not to bring this cartoon along because it would hurt your feelings, but I did it

anyway." Then I pulled it out of the envelope.

Nixon laughed. "You know, Art," he commented, "I recall that cartoon very well. It was reprinted in the *New York Times* in the 'News of the Week' section on Sunday,"—and he spieled off the exact date. I didn't recall the date myself, but when I got home I looked it up. He was right on the button. What a memory!

Nixon was a strange melange—a tragic-comic figure who, despite his multiple talents and ability, seemed to be his own worst enemy, bent on self-destruction. But whatever the political judgment, he will be remembered forever for his sensational ski-nose, his heavy beard, and his drooping jowls—the ideal subject for any red-blooded American cartoonist.

In 1976, I was elected President of the Association of American Editorial Cartoonists. Gerald Ford, who had just become president of the United States upon Nixon's resignation, was extremely popular on both sides of the aisle on Capitol Hill, but practically unknown to cartoonists. Even his home state cartoonists, Arthur Poinier of the *Detroit News* and Frank Williams of the *Detroit Free Press,* had rarely featured him in their cartoons.

Shortly after the swearing-in ceremony on the capitol steps, plans were set in motion to again put together a collection of cartoons especially drawn for the new president. I had arrived at the White House with an elaborate book of drawings for President Ford that had been put together by the Merkle Press. It contained over 100 caricatures of the president— the largest compilation of drawings ever contributed by the political cartoonists of the country.

The White House guard gave a loud sigh as he lifted the bulky wrapped book to place it and the framed certificate of honorary membership on the scanning machine, a security measure with any package entering the White House.

"This is the heaviest object we have had on the machine since I have been here," he said. "What in the world is in it?"

"Gold bars," I responded, then quickly explained that the weighty object was a book

White House photo

The author (left) introducing Ed Fischer, Milt Morris, Jack Jurden, and Gene Payne to President Gerald Ford.

of cartoons. Cartoonists had flown in from all over the country for the presentation.

"The president has been briefed," Press Secretary Ron Nessen said, "but he is looking to you to introduce each one." And then we went into the Oval office to meet President Ford.

The president personally greeted and visited with each cartoonist. Ed Fischer of the *Omaha World-Herald* had done a special cartoon showing a statue being erected at the president's birthplace in Omaha, which amused Ford. The cartoon featured an equestrian statue of Ford complete with football helmet, a detail which the president noted with a loud guffaw.

"I will look at all of them later," he said, "so thank each member who contributed." He then put the book down on the sofa and turned toward a small anteroom, right off the Oval Office. "Now come and let me show you my framed cartoon collection," he beckoned. The small office had been used by Rose Mary Wood during the Nixon days, and the room had been redecorated. The walls were covered with original cartoons and mementoes. In the middle of one wall was a framed picture of Ford's winning Michigan football team, with the president prominently pictured in the center of the picture in the appropriate field position. Cartoonist John Stampone, who had trouble seeing, asked, "Mr. President, where are you in the picture?" This set off a loud round of laughter. The president took him up close to point out where he was in the picture.

From the small room President Ford took the group into his working office to show off a beautiful mahogany desk that had belonged to President James Monroe. Mrs. Ford had rediscovered the desk and had had it refinished. Gib Crockett of the *Washington Star,* who is an expert furniture-maker himself, commented on the type of mahogany and the manner in which it was put together. President Ford seemed impressed. The president used the desk to sign a few mementoes, and the rest of the time was spent visiting informally with the cartoonists.

Our meeting with Jimmy Carter was an up-and-down affair. As with former chief executives, the Association of American Editorial Cartoonists prepared a book of original cartoons for President Carter. Before putting it together, we had checked with the White House to see if the present would be welcomed. Assured that it would indeed be acceptable, the group went ahead and put together a book of presidential caricatures.

On its completion, we touched base with the White House press office to determine an appropriate time to make the presentation. Calls and letters by the dozen were sent to 1600 Pennsylvania Avenue over a period of months, but all was quiet on the White House front. No one returned the calls or answered the mail. Our letters seemingly found their way to the White House dead-letter box. No other administration had ever acted in this manner, and we began to suspect that the president, or his staff, or both, had little use for cartoons or cartoonists.

Finally, Press Aide Rex Granum agreed to a preliminary meeting, but after a pleasant visit and a chance to see the president and Mrs. Carter off in the helicopter to Camp David,

another period of silence set in. It was not until Georgia cartoonist Baldy (Cliff Baldowski) of the *Atlanta Constitution* visited in Atlanta with Gerald Rafshoon, assistant to the president for communications, and told him of the long delay, was a date fixed.

Jerry Robinson, president of the Association of American Editorial Cartoonists, makes a humorous point to another president, Jimmy Carter.

On Wednesday, October 11, 1978, at 11:30 A.M., the cartoonists were ushered into the Oval Office, but the president was not at his desk. In a few minutes he opened the door and peeked into the room. "Is it safe?" he asked with a grin. After greeting each artist, he was presented with the AAEC album and an illuminated membership scroll. He reminisced about his favorite political cartoon from the Athens, Georgia, newspaper—the original of which he said was hanging in his kitchen at home. It concerned the devil with a pitchfork aimed at the then-governor running for president and holding a snowball, with the devil saying, "I'm betting on the snowball."

The president said that he received a press compilation of cartoons once a week— "whenever I want to be depressed"—but added that cartoonists contribute much to the historical record of the nation, and that he followed their work even when they were

White House photo

President Ronald Reagan offers the author a warm White House welcome.

vicious, which he seemed to imply was a regular, if not daily, characteristic of the trade.

He signed a blowup of the caricature I had contributed to the album, but said he would only autograph that *one.* I was glad to be the first in line. When we said "Thank you, Mr. President," he seemed much relieved.

The meeting with President Reagan in May of 1982 was different in tone and atmosphere. He seemed to relish cartoons and indicated an enthusiasm and interest much like that of President Truman. He chatted amiably with cartoonists in the group and was photograped shaking hands with each one. I had not met the president before, and he looked years younger and taller than I had expected from viewing

him on television. He was nattily dressed in a blue pin-stripe suit and stood erect but relaxed. He laughed at the cartoons in the book and paged through the entire volume, pointing out the attending artists' work. He then showed us his cartoon collection framed on a wall adjoining the Oval Office. Many of the drawings had been done for him following the assassination attempt and were "get-well" cards. Others were political cartoons. President Reagan likes to draw and frequently doodles at cabinet meetings. He is an avid cartoon fan, following the comics as well as political cartoons. We all were pleased to have a budding cartoonist in the White House.

27

"Advice fo' Chillun"

AL CAPP for many years used as a topper (a supplementary feature run above the main comic) for *Li'l Abner* a panel entitled "Advice fo' Chillun." It really wasn't for children, but rather was directed to the general public. It was humorous and colloquial and contained friendly advice on a number of subjects. In this chapter I will try to match Capp's helpful suggestions.

The question most commonly asked cartoonists is "How do you get your ideas?" A close second is "How do you get a job as a cartoonist?" In between are sandwiched many queries on technique and reproduction.

The trait most valuable for anyone going into the art business is persistence—dogged persistence. Cartooning is not a profession for the fainthearted. If you are easily discouraged, forget it. In order to qualify, one must have a modicum of talent with an ability to look at life in a creative manner and to transpose ideas onto paper in a way that attracts the public's eye. Like show business, the art field is tough and competitive. There are only several hundred comic artists in the U.S. and about the same number of political cartoonists—a narrow spectrum indeed. To make matters worse, space in today's newspapers is limited, and to sell a feature requires bumping a feature already in print and with a following. In addition, the comics have become spe-

cialized, directed to a particular theme or audience—a strip for the retirees, the teenagers, particular professions, or political groups—something for every persuasion.

Syndication has been both the making and breaking of the cartoonist. Widespread distribution of an artist's work by a sales-oriented organization brings increased income to the artist, but at the same time restricts the profession by reducing or eliminating jobs. This is particularly true in political cartooning where traditionally the cartoonist has been based at a specific newspaper. If picked up by a syndicate, his work not only appears in the artist's home newspaper, but is sold to large and small papers across the nation and overseas. A package rate is established based on the circulation of the paper purchasing the work. Rates are high for a big-city daily and low for a small rural daily or weekly paper. As a result, newspapers can subscribe to an artist's work for a nominal sum, and many papers buy the work of three or four or more editorial cartoonists, choosing which cartoons the editor wants to run on the editorial or op-ed page. This makes it most difficult for young cartoonists to land a job, as an editor can buy the work of top professionals for much less than hiring a staff cartoonist. Of course, local cartoons have a tremendous impact, and a syndicate service cannot provide local cartoons on a national scale. The local cartoon is a very popular commodity, ranking at the highest levels of readership. For this reason many papers prefer to have their own cartoonist present a view sympathetic to that of the newspaper or an independent view to stimulate public interest.

Some cartoonists prefer to work only with a syndicate as it gives greater editorial freedom and a more independent political view since the artist (not his editor) calls the tune.

There has always been tension between editor and political cartoonist. The editorials and the editorial cartoon vie for space and attention, often running side by side on the page. Most editors are anxious for the cartoon to supplement their words of wisdom, and some executives pressure the cartoonist to either relate to the lead editorial or to hew closely to the paper's policy. It has been traditional for the cartoonist to work for and with the editor, and in most cases the editor has the final say as to which idea is chosen and used. Consequently, there often is fierce competition between the two. In recent years the tendency has been to give the cartoonist free rein to act as his own man in expressing his opinion, as would any columnist. After all, the cartoonist signs his cartoon, and it is the output of his creative genius and political leaning. Therefore publishers have been more lenient in permitting the cartoonist to do his work with fewer limitations or restrictions. As a consequence, the political cartoon in America has taken on a renewed spirit of independence. The result is a more vibrant product.

Editors serve as useful sounding boards and in many cases can sharpen an idea or caption. At the very least, they can check the spelling and advise on policy matters. In many cases editor and cartoonist work together smoothly as a team.

The most important ingredient of the cartoon is the idea. Everyone wants to know where you get ideas and the magic formula for coming up with a blockbuster every day. The truth is the cartoonist does not produce a gem every day, but most do manage to churn out a remarkable number of crowd-pleasers. Sur-

prisingly, many ideas the artist thinks are his weakest turn out to be the most popular with the general public. Often drawings done rapidly are the most famous of an artist's career. John T. McCutcheon's "Mysterious Stranger" was drawn in less than a half-hour, and "Ding" Darling's hastily constructed cartoon on the death of Theodore Roosevelt, "The Long Long Trail," was most memorable.

Let me say at the outset that I firmly believe ideas are a gift of God. The Bible tells us that there are many gifts (I Cor. 12: 4–11), and one is a creative mind. There are some people who have a special ability to visualize situations in a humorous or profound manner. There is an ease and naturalness about the process of coming up with ideas that others, no matter how hard they try, are not able to achieve. This is a gift, and should be considered so. There are methods, however, of stimulating thoughts that can help the creative process along. These vary with every artist, and nailing down a particular system for producing ideas is difficult and elusive. Suffice it to say, the artist must select a subject that is in the news now or soon will be. In a way, he molds the news with his pen and frequently foresees events about to occur.

The usual process is to select three or four subjects of primary interest, listing them in order of their importance. This is an advantage over the gag cartoonist who has to be funny with a blank piece of drawing paper on his board and no particular subject in mind. At least the political cartoonist has puppets to play with on his stage, and he can arrange the strings to his liking. Timeliness is of the essence. A cartoon idea must endure long enough for the paper or papers using the drawing to run it without it becoming obsolete in the first edition. That means the artist must be ahead of the news to the extent that his commentary is current and pertinent. This is particularly true of the syndicated cartoonist, whose work is distributed through the mail. One hopes the cartoon will be good for at least two or three days.

After the cartoonist has decided which subject or subjects he plans to "hit," he then tries to come up with an original concept to best illustrate the news. This could be a reworking of an already familiar idea or an excursion in a new direction entirely—perhaps a surprise twist, some unexpected or different concept from the one the reader would normally expect. If the subject calls for a humorous approach, the artist will lean in that direction. Conversely, a death or assassination requires a serious or more dramatic rendering. The subject decides the mood while the artist manipulates the staging.

One technique is to reach back into history or literature to find a similar pattern or situation, a parking lot where the artist can maneuver his vehicle. Perhaps the model won't fit into the particular space available, but it gives the driver a good opportunity to see what interesting antique cars are on the block. Perhaps one will strike his fancy. A good education in the liberal arts is a plus for anyone in the graphics. During the late 1800s and well into the early 1900s, cartoonists used classical allegories to picture current issues. The Bible, Shakespeare, Dante, Milton, Chaucer, and others were common sources. Today the decline in the study of the classics, both in high school and at the college level, has made it

difficult for young people to understand classical allusions. Consequently the cartoonists lean to widely known references, avoiding mythology and Biblical illustrations unless the themes are commonplace—Noah and the Ark, David and Goliath, Hamlet, and Romeo and Juliet.

Another method is to make good use of familiar symbols, such as Uncle Sam. The public "has grown accustomed to his face," and any use of Uncle Sam or his distant relatives— John Bull, Columbia, Dame France—or his pets, such as the dove of peace, the Democratic donkey, the Republican elephant, the Tammany tiger, or the Thanksgiving turkey, brings immediate smiles of recognition and appreciation from the masses. Purists in recent years have played down and ridiculed the overuse of such symbols, but like it or not, if the cartoonist neglects to feature familiar faces he will get a strong negative response from readers who like and expect to see those symbols they have loved and accepted over the years.

Innovative cartoonists such as Pat Oliphant have continued to use the standard symbols but have changed them to suit their own styles and liking. Oliphant's Uncle Sam closely resem-

'WE BELIEVE THE LIL' FELLAS LONG FOR A CHANCE TO EXPERIENCE DEMOCRACY AND THE ELECTORAL PROCESS AS WE KNOW IT.'

'AH, YES, INDEED — REMINDS ME OF THE TIME I WAS IN VIETNAM. I HAD TRAINED AND ARMED THE GOVERNMENT TROOPS, AND WAS SURROUNDED BY HOSTILES...'

bles a chubby, cryptic W. C. Fields. Others have personalized the Bomb or substituted Chicken Little for the dove of peace.

A method for working up ideas used by gag cartoonists is that of word-or-picture-association. The use of three-by-five-inch cards is helpful. One group of cards may list various types of persons or professions: Eskimos, tourists, windowwashers, or bankers. Another group of cards may have specific activities: surfing, running, thinking, diving, or driving a car. The cards are shuffled, and one from each deck is selected and matched. For instance, eskimos—surfing. The cartoonist then tries to think up a gag to match the situation.

Poring through picture books or magazines often triggers ideas, as a painting or photograph will suggest some related activities or subjects which can be utilized by a facile mind.

Another way to reach the reader with ideas that are relevant is to relate the cartoon to some subject of current colloquial interest—a popular movie, a top song, a widely followed television show, or some community event appealing to the local audience. Public speakers utilize this technique to good advantage in the introductory part of their speeches, referring to local people or places known to the audience. The first priority with a speaker on the circuit is to carefully read the local press for such angles. This usually adds a personal touch to the presentation. It also works with the cartoon.

After the idea is nailed down, it becomes necessary to get down to the technical side. What equipment is necessary? What types of pens and brushes are best? How about the paper? Basic equipment would include a good ruler, a compass (a compass set is more desirable), some good erasers (preferably kneaded), pencils of varying softness, a drawing board, paper, and artists' tape or thumbtacks. The drawing board can be as simple as a regular kitchen bread board. For beginners, this probably is best. If interest is maintained, a more elaborate board can be purchased at a later date.

Pens and brushes depend upon the style and pleasure of the artist. Some artists prefer a fine spencerian pen, others a broader point. Any art store can advise you on its stock. Hunt 512 or 513 are good pens for starters, as is an Esterbrook 358. Brushes should be of good quality. Try Winsor & Newton or Grumbacher numbers 2, 3, or 4.

A number of cartoonists have switched from regular drawing pens to a felt pen or its equivalent, because it is easy to use, free-flowing, and quick. The Design Art markers (Eberhard Faber) come in varying widths—ultra-fine, fine, and pointed nib. They are quick drying, handy to use, and rather reasonable. While black is standard for reproduction, these pens also come in colors that can be whited over with "Chinese White" without bleeding in the event corrections have to be made. One disadvantage of these quick-drying pens is that the drawing can turn a bluish color if water or dampness touches the paper. Regular felt pens also run or blot if water comes in contact with the ink.

A good opaque watercolor for use on paper or acetate with pen, brush, or airbrush is PRO White. Higgins and Pelikan make excellent India inks that keep a rich blackness on the original. A number of cartoonists, particularly the gag cartoonists who are submitting roughs or preliminary drawings for approval, use plain bond paper. The 8½-by-11-inch size is convenient for mailing in standard envelopes. Strathmore drawing board is widely used and comes in varying widths or weights of ply. Any paper that takes ink well will do.

Ohio Graphic Arts Systems, Inc., of Warren Heights, Ohio, is the only company that makes Grafix uni-shade or duo-shade paper. This pre-printed and prepared paper features two hidden shades of light and dark lines that can be brought out by the application of two acids (one for each shade) supplied by the manufacturer. This gives a tone or shading to the drawing when applied to the original by use of a special brush. A similar method of adding a grey tone to the original is ben-day, a wax paper covered with pre-printed dots of varying patterns. This is cut to fit the areas where shading is desired. The wax sticks to the drawing when pressed down. Art shops stock many varieties of this adhesive.

Other papers have pebbled surfaces and are usually referred to as coquille board. A crayon or black pencil is needed to bring out the pattern. A polycromos (60 or 199) Castell black made by A. W. Faber is one of the best. An ordinary hardware marking crayon can also be used, as can a lithograph crayon. A lithograph crayon cannot be erased as can the polycromos pencil. It also has a slick surface and does not take touch-up white without great effort.

The size of the original drawing can vary greatly. Some artists are more comfortable working in a large format, while others work in very small size and in some cases the exact size of the reproduction in the paper or magazine.

Standard size for political cartoons is 9-by-10½-inches for vertical cartoons and nine-by-fifteen-inches for horizontal cartoons. Comic strip originals are usually 5¼-inches high by 18 inches wide. However, many artists use a full sheet of drawing paper or illustration board.

In political cartoons there are taboos from editor to editor. Most editors shy away from snakes since readers often have an abhorrence of them. The use of profanity or foreign words is usually avoided. Paul Szep of the *Boston Globe* once used a Russian word to give the cartoon a Soviet flavor, and it turned out to be a coarse obscenity. He was suspended for several weeks for this *faux pas*. Care has to be taken with Chinese or Japanese characters to make certain they are not unwittingly offensive. Care also should be taken not to make fun

of religious groups or church symbols. And curse words are avoided by the use of substitutes—stars, exclamation points, asterisks, and curlycues. Other areas skirted are double entendre or sexual references, or the use of specific numbers on license plates. I was sued for making the error of putting numbers in the license plate of a car in a highway safety cartoon on drunk driving. The cartoon showed a drunk with bottle in hand weaving in and out of traffic. The car was shaped like a pig and the caption was "Road Hog." The random number I used turned out to be the plate of a well-known individual. My paper had to pay!

Procedures for getting a job as a political cartoonist or comic artist differ because of the nature of the business. Most political cartoonists work for individual newspapers while comic artists work for syndicates.

In editorial cartooning, the artist has to go where the work is. The first step will be to determine which papers do not have a staff cartoonist. This information can be obtained by consulting the *Editor and Publisher Yearbook,* which lists the staffs of all the leading papers by state and city. It also gives the circulation of the papers. While there are exceptions, a good rule of thumb is that a paper will need a circulation of 100,000 to afford a staff man. If the artist prefers a particular part of the country, he can focus on papers in a given area. Make a list of all the papers without staffers and then select those editorial pages which appeal to you and match your politics. Then get copies of the paper at an out-of-town newsstand or subscribe to the paper for a limited period. Study the editorials of the paper to determine policy and the way the news is played. Develop three or four cartoons based on this study. With these finished cartoons—your best effort—in hand, you are ready to contact the paper.

From my experience, personal contact is best. Make an appointment to see the editor or editorial-page editor. Dress neatly and be on time. You are your own best salesman, so without being obtrusive, promote your work and its value to that paper. Stress the advantage of local cartoons over syndicated work. If you are good at caricature or courtroom sketching, emphasize these talents. If the editor expresses interest but does not have an opening at the moment, keep in touch without being a pest. Persistence pays off.

Another procedure is to put together a brochure of your best work and mail it to those papers without a cartoonist. Include a picture and a brief biographical sketch, and, if possible, some quotes by fellow cartoonists or local leaders praising your work. Include a return address and phone number.

You can also advertise in the trade journals: *Editor and Publisher, The Quill* (the organ of Sigma Delta Chi, the professional journalism society), and other publications read by editors. A short advertisement can bring prompt results if a newspaper is looking for a cartoonist.

Telephone calls to editors will probably be given short shrift.

In displaying your work, limit the output to a dozen drawings at the most. The editor's time is valuable, and he can get a good idea after inspecting only a few cartoons. Put your favorite ones on top and be sure they are your best. Be sure the lettering is clean and legible. A sure sign of amateur work is poor lettering. Study the lettering of the top cartoonists and synthesize their techniques.

Selling comic strips and panels requires a somewhat different approach from that of the political cartoon. Syndicates receive thousands of submissions a week, and your work must be professional and properly packaged to catch the editor's eye. To sell a comic strip or panel, your idea must be striking and must appeal to a specific segment of the public. As mentioned earlier, comics are directed to a particular audience, the elderly, the Pepsi Generation, space-age enthusiasts, and so forth. Spend the most time developing the concept and the cast of characters. Rough up a

month or so of daily strips and two or three for the Sunday pages. Do a scenario of what you intend to accomplish with the strip. Develop a character study of each personality in the strip. Put it in writing beside sketches of the character in varying positions to give the editor an insight into your thinking. It is much like casting a play.

If yours is a humor strip, select the best gags and do "finishes" of them—ink a dozen, or a two-week supply. Also complete one Sunday page and have several others penciled in. Be sure the lettering is not overcrowded and that it is easy to read. Do not write a book in the balloons. Remember the reduction problem. When you have finished the artwork, have the drawings photostated. Most printing houses can do this work for you.

It is a good idea to have the original drawings reduced to the size they appear in the paper, both daily and Sunday. Have several sets made since you may need to submit them to more than one syndicate. *Never* submit original artwork. If lost, your project will go down the drain.

Coloring the Sunday-page photostat with watercolors is a nice touch.

Editor and Publisher also prints a yearly syndicate directory which lists management names and syndicate addresses. You can either mail the work to the comic editor or, if the office is in your area, pay a personal visit.

Friends can be very important. If you know a cartoonist, consult him or her for tips on what the syndicate is looking for at the time. A good word helps if your cartoonist friend is impressed with your work. Contacts *are* important, and, combined with talent and perseverance, can make it possible for you to snag the golden ring on the cartoon merry-go-round.

28

Ghosts
and Other Secrets

THERE IS a thin line separating the comic strip and the political cartoon. The greatest difference is in the structure and placement. The political cartoon traditionally has been in a panel shape—square or rectangular—appearing on the front page of the paper or on the editorial page, while the comic strip is usually horizontal with sequential panels forming the idea or gag. Most comics have been just that— either humorous situations or adventure strips, utilizing essentially the same format. Panel cartoons, such as George Lichty's *Grin and Bear It* or Hank Ketcham's *Dennis The Menace,* are sandwiched between the comic strips or arranged at the bottom of the page for variety. Most papers place the comics at the back of the feature page or toward the end of the classified sections. Occasionally they are placed in other parts of the paper, but this is usually for topical reasons—a sports cartoon for the sports page, a woman's cartoon for the woman's page, and so forth.

Subject matter, however, often overlaps. Many comic strips intrude into the political realm. Harold Gray's *Little Orphan Annie* espoused Republican philosophy, while Walt Kelly's *Pogo* usually took a liberal bend. Both ridiculed the political arena in general.

Al Capp used *Li'l Abner* to savagely satirize both sides of the fence. Early in his career he made fun of the conservatives, such as Senator Jack S. Phogbound, and later the liberals, calling them "smug and sanctimonious." Folk singer Joan Baez he dubbed "Joanie Phoanie,"

LITTLE ORPHAN ANNIE

Harold Gray; *Little Orphan Annie*—reprinted by permission: Tribune Media Services

and the college protesters he labeled S.W.I.N.E.—Students Wildly Indignant About Nearly Everything. Gary Trudeau's *Doonesbury* won a Pulitzer Prize for his political commentary in the popular strip.

Many of the panel cartoons, such as Jim Berry's *Berry's World,* while considered comic strips by genre, are actually political in nature, featuring current leaders of government and world figures.

Conversely, political cartoonists utilize the comics in their editorial cartoons if the occasion warrants. So many editorial cartoonists were drawing *Peanuts* characters in their cartoons that Charles Schulz protested, saying his creations were being used in a political orientation of which he did not approve. This did not slow down the use of his characters, however, with the usual "Apologies to Charles Schulz" penned at the bottom of the political cartoon.

A battle that both comic and political cartoonists fight is that of space. With the rise in the cost of newsprint and the ever-increasing importance of advertisements to pay the freight, space is at a premium. This has been accentuated as newspapers shrink due to mergers or closings.

Sunday comics have been reduced from full-page size, to one-half page, to one-third page, to one-fourth page, and the daily strips have been crammed together to conserve space. Consequently, fans, particularly the older ones, have difficulty reading the features. It has placed an undue burden on the artists as well. Beautifully drawn adventure strips such as Hal Foster's *Prince Valiant* and Milton Caniff's *Steve Canyon* have been forced to resort to closeups and heavy use of blacks to be clearly visible. Intricate battle scenes force the Shakespearian ruse of having the action off stage. As a result, there has been a greater emphasis on the simply drawn gag strip with more white space and larger lettering. The text, as well as the drawing, suffers.

When Walt Kelly's *Pogo* was dropped, Al Capp had this to say:

> The death of "Pogo" is an irreparable loss to American art and humor. Few times in the history of both arts has there emerged a man like Walt Kelly, who could write as exquisitely as he could draw. The closest the English ever came to that was Lewis Carroll's "Alice," but that had to be illustrated by Sir John Tenniel.
>
> Kelly, however, left us with one phrase that says more about the state of our newspapers than any editorialist: "We have met the enemy," said Kelly, "and he is us."
>
> I read with disbelief that Kelly's peak of 300 newspapers had dwindled, in under 15 years, to 150 newspapers. Was "Pogo" any less good 5 years ago than it was 10 or 20 years ago? It was as rare, and as healthy. Then why didn't newspapers, who rate the value of their comic strips by polls, notice that Kelly was falling further and further behind? Do as many editors read comic strips as read polls? Didn't they notice that as the space they gave to comics diminished, the readership of strips like "Pogo" dropped off? The strips were as good as they'd ever been and, in Kelly's case, as good as anything in American humor had ever been. But readers simply COULD NOT SEE THEM. Asking Walt Kelly to create "Pogo" in the asphyxiating space generally given to him was like asking John Steinbeck to write *Grapes of Wrath* on the back of an envelope.

Other artists have expressed a similar view. Roy Crane (*Buz Sawyer*) complained that "the new strip sizes allow the artists to draw only heads and shoulders of their characters. There's no action in strips, because there's no space." Chester Gould (*Dick Tracy*) commented, "Newspapers don't have to commit suicide. All they have to do is start being newspapers again instead of trying to be television sets. . . . The daily cartoon strip was newspapers' visual show long, long before TV, and it's still the hottest feature in the newspaper. Why do editors put this dynamic salesman in a coffin 2 by 6 inches and hide him in the back room?"

The political cartoon has not fared quite as badly, although cartoons run at one time on the front page of newspapers and often in color have been moved deep inside to the editorial or op-ed pages. Fortunately a number of editors recognize the fact that if you can't see it you won't read it, and have given more space to the political cartoon.

STEVE CANYON

Milton Caniff; *Steve Canyon*—reprinted with special permission of King Features Syndicate, Inc.

Another casualty of "the battle for inner space" not recognized by the general public is that large portions of the Sunday pages are deleted to fit the half-page or one-third-page formats.

The artist must arrange the sequence of his cartoon so that a number of panels can be dropped without affecting the storyline. Usually the title and next panel are sacrificed and are designed to be self-contained and can be eliminated by tabloid newspapers. This is called a "throwaway." Another panel is cut to bridge the action and line-up the page. This is referred to as a "transitional panel."

The public is not usually aware of another facet of the cartoon, ghosting. Turning out 365 cartoons a year is a gargantuan task. The artist is not given the privilege of getting sick or taking a vacation. That hole *must* be filled every day. Most features run for a number of years. To enable the artist to have an occasional breather from this terrific pressure, help is called in. This can be either on the art side or on the writing side. These helpers or assistants are called "ghosts" because they usually do not sign the work. Only the name of the creator appears on the feature. In recent years some artists have credited their ghosts by letting them sign the cartoons under or beside their names.

Some comic artists do a number of strips. Mort Walker leads the pack with five—*Beetle Bailey, Hi and Lois, Boner's Ark, Sam and Silo,* and *The Evermores.* Several artists—such as Mell Lazarus, Brant Parker, and Johnny Hart—do two strips. Naturally the sheer number requires a helping hand. Collabora-

tion is becoming a natural phenomenon in the comics. It is irreverently referred to as "the factory syndrome." Few political cartoonists have used ghosts. Hearst cartoonist Burris Jenkins, Jr., used one. So did Rube Goldberg. Goldberg's ghost, Warren King, later became a well-known cartoonist with the *New York Daily News.*

In the early days of cartooning most artists worked at their respective newspapers. That has changed. Today the trend is toward working at a home studio. This permits the cartoonist to avoid the long trips into the city and traffic tieups. The work can be delivered by messenger or through the mail. Bill Mauldin has a teletype machine in his home and his cartoons are sent out over the wire. Time is money.

29

The Cartoon as Art

THE CARTOON has been termed "America's only original contribution to the world of art." The value of the cartoon as an art form, a vital historical record, and a commentary of our own times is generally recognized by historians and art scholars.

Some of the most renowned artists of the past were, in reality, cartoonists. Often they were considered in their own lifetimes "lowbrow," "vulgar," and out of step with the times, when in fact the exact opposite was true. Many of the European artists who were occupied with cartooning in one phase or another were ridiculed as being pseudo-artists, imposters, and often worse. But as the years have passed, we find that many of these men were indeed among the outstanding artists of their time.

Names which immediately come to mind are Daumier, Goya, Hogarth, Cruikshank, Toulouse-Lautrec, Dore, Blake, Forain, and Kley. One of the most important contributions of the cartoonist is as an historian. He is a chronicler of the times in which he lives and a most effective critic and commentator. He must summarize an event quickly, simply, and with impact. It is for this reason that the work of the cartoonist has been an important factor in the development of the nation. Open any history book or text and one will find it profusely illustrated with cartoons. These cartoons trace significant incidents from the founding of the colonies to the present administration. Cartoons vividly portray history and men who made history.

The first American political cartoonist was among the most noted of our founding fathers. What student can forget the dramatic "Join, or Die" cartoon, penned by Benjamin Franklin in the *Pennsylvania Gazette* in 1754? Frank Luther Mott, in a treatise on American journalism, said,

> The first American newspaper cartoon was that of a divided snake. This was based on the popular superstition that a snake that had been cut in two would come to life if the pieces were joined before sunset. It showed a snake in eight pieces representing as many colonial governments, with the legend "Join, or Die." It immediately caught the public fancy and was reproduced in other papers.

"Join, or Die" became the rallying cry of the colonies, and the cartoon was used as a basis for one of this nation's first flags. In December of 1775 *Bradford's Journal* commented:

> Perhaps the most popular symbol of the time was a rattlesnake, together with the slogan "Don't Tread on Me." On one banner we find the coiled serpent added to the pine tree design. This choice was explained by a contemporary writer as follows: The rattlesnake's eye was brighter than any other animal, she has no eyelids and thus might be

taken as a symbol of vigilance, and furthermore she never began an attack, but never surrendered when assailed. Most important, the bite of the rattlesnake was deadly. "It is curious and amazing to observe how distinct and independent of each other the rattles of this reptile are, and yet how firmly united together. One of these rattles, singly, is incapable of producing a sound, but the ringing of thirteen together is sufficient to alarm the boldest man living."

Other well-known contemporary names in the cartoon field were Paul Revere, James Akin, and Gilbert Stuart. Each period of our history has produced famous cartoonists to outline a dramatic picture of the time.

The first political cartoon, as we think of it today, was drawn by the celebrated portrait painter John Wesley Jarvis in 1814 for the *New York Evening Post*. It was entitled "Death of the Embargo," depicting Pres. James Madison.

Cartoons in the early days of this country were usually partisan and often venomous, perhaps reaching their zenith at the time of Lincoln.

Lincoln was depicted by the opposition as a tall, grotesque oaf, receiving counsel from Satan and smearing the Constitution with his huge, gawky feet. In a caricature in *Vanity Fair*, Lincoln was portrayed as being so frightened of assassination that he disguised himself in a Scottish cape and cap upon entering Washington. Nothing was shown of Lincoln but the cap and two feet protruding from the long flowing cape. Despite this vilification, President Lincoln recognized the importance of the cartoon and the vital role it played: "Thomas Nast has been our best recruiting sergeant," said Lincoln near the close of the Civil War. "His emblematic cartoons have never failed to arouse enthusiasm and patriotism, and have always seemed to come just when these articles were getting scarce."

By the time of Theodore Roosevelt, the cartoonists had grown in number and influence. The robust president's toothy grin and pince-nez glasses were drawn by countless newspaper artists whose work was seen on a broader scale because of improvements in the techniques of printing. Caricatures of Roosevelt were collected and filled two entire volumes. C. K. Berryman of the *Washington Star* added a mascot to his cartoons, a little bear which he had nicknamed "Teddy" in honor of the hunting exploits of the president. And so was born the Teddy Bear—one of the most popular symbols in the nation's history.

World War I brought to the attention of the country some of the most powerful artists in the history of cartooning: Oscar Cesare, Perry Carter, Louis Raemaekers, Bruce Bairnsfather, Boardman Robinson, Rollin Kirby, Herbert Johnson, and H. T. Webster, to name but a few. As mentioned earlier, the *New York Times*, one of the most influential papers in the nation, once a week devoted an entire page to a single cartoon by its noted caricaturist, Edwin Marcus.

The cartoon molded public opinion and brought the era into focus. Cartoons were drawn with force and power, and the works of the artists of this period compare favorably with the best of Daumier. Fitzpatrick and Weed, Darling and Minor, Talburt and Seibel, Orr and Kirby drew cartoons that rocked the nation both artistically and emotionally. The *New York Times* has said of Daniel Fitzpatrick:

> He believes, with Goethe, in light, more light. His way of shedding it is understandable in any language. All surplus jiggling lines and meaningless blobs of drawing are eliminated. A Fitzpatrick cartoon may be jubilant about politics, but it is usually above it, deeply about human beings but never below their stature.

World War II also brought into focus many noted artists depicting "man's inhumanity to man." Bill Mauldin's *Up Front* cartoons give a more graphic picture of war than almost any artist since Goya. The same can be said for the political drawings of Howard Brodie, Gilbert Bundy, and John Groth, which were done under fire on the front lines. Here again, the leading political commentators in the realm of the cartoon served their nation well. Who can forget the powerful anti-Axis cartoons of Edmund Duffy, Arthur Szyk, David Low, Antonio Arias Bernal, Herblock, Ross Lewis,

Vaughn Shoemaker, C. D. Batchelor, Cy Hungerford, and Bruce Russell? And on a more contemporary note, despots and dictators continue to tremble before the slashing pen of the editorial cartoonist. At the 1979 Moscow International Book Fair, a prestigious event in the publishing world, five editions of *Best Editorial Cartoons of the Year* were confiscated by Soviet authorities and removed from the exhibition hall. The book, published annually by Pelican Publishing Company since 1973, features the best works of some 140 cartoonists. The cartoons were considered dangerous to Marxist ideology.

In a peculiar defense of the action, the chairman of the Soviet State Publishing Committee insisted: "It is not correct to say that (this action) is a violation of freedom of speech. It is the highest affirmation of freedom of speech." Apparently the reasoning of Soviet officials—at least those who have been provoked by cartoons—is not subject to the normal standards of common sense.

The incident prompted syndicated columnist Art Buchwald to observe: "What do the Russians fear from us the most? It's not our cruise missiles, our nuclear submarines, our B-52 bombers, or our new MX system. They're afraid of our books . . . including five editions of the *Best Editorial Cartoons*."

Today, the political cartoonist continues *his* war against the forces of evil—whether local, national, or international. Day in and day out the cartoonist mirrors history; he reduces complex facts into understandable and artistic terminology. He is a political commentator and at the same time an artist. For this reason, the cartoon becomes a continuing and necessary adjunct of our culture. Like the hieroglyphics and cuneiform of ancient times, it is a pictorial review of history. Cartoons have always commented upon the frailities of the human being. This is in essence the true purpose of the cartoon. The cartoon sheds a bright light on the inner darkness of the soul. Often this light is accompanied by considerable heat, as in the work of the great English caricaturist George Cruikshank.

The social artist attempts in his work to emulate the "sparkling crystallization of all that is great in Cruikshank's work: *Joie de vivre,* a watchmaker's eye for detail, a penetrating but nevertheless sympathetic insight to Everyman's foibles, and brilliant caricature."

In the early days of this country, social satire was featured in the many humorous weeklies or comic almanacs inspired by *Cruikshank's Almanac,* which was amply illustrated with the publisher's own cartoons. In the United States, the earliest satirical magazine, *The American Comic Almanac,* appeared in Boston in 1831. Shortly thereafter (1835), another comic almanac was published in Tennessee. It was entitled *Davy Crockett's Almanac or Sports of the Old West* and made effective use of the cartoon. A more sophisticated approach to humor appeared in the publication *Puck,* founded by the noted engraver and political cartoonist, Joseph Keppler, in the late 1870s. *Puck* combined social commentary and political ridicule. It employed a staff of regular cartoonists much like *The New Yorker* of today. Other periodicals soon followed, most notably *Judge* in 1881 and *Life* in 1883. Thomas Craven, in *Cartoon Cavalcade,* noted,

> From these pioneering journals, one might glean some choice specimens of uncouth jesting, genuine to the core and still fragrant, and an equal number of refined authentic pleasantries in the English manner. . . . It is enough to say that the volume of comic drawings mounted impressively as the century waned, and the production from 1900 to the present had been beyond any man's capacity for enjoyment.

Among the noted artists working for these publications were M. A. Woolf, with his fiercely tragic drawings of the poor; T. S. Sullivant, with his hilarious animal drawings in a parody of the middle class; and Charles Dana Gibson, with his magnificent pen portraits of the upper strata of society. These penetrating studies of the American public were all-inclusive.

Other gifted artists of social satire were Frederick Opper, E. W. Kemble, R. F. Outcault, L. M. Glackens, H. MacGill, T. E. Powers, and Art Young.

Today, despite the rise of syndication and the popular humorous panel cartoons which appear in newspapers throughout the country, the very best of social commentary still is found in a weekly magazine, *The New Yorker.* This magazine, one of the most literate publications in the United States, uses *only* cartoons as illustrations. Here is found perhaps the best and most pungent social commentary in the world. Such artists as James Thurber and Helen Hokinson worked exclusively for this publication. The satiric drawings of Saul Steinberg, Whitney Darrow, Jr., O. Soglow, Chon Day, Richard Taylor, Gluyas Williams, Peter Arno, Alan Dunn, Abner Dean, Charles Addams, Alajalov, Rea Irving, Mary Petty, Richter, William Steig, Carl Rose, George Price, and Ludwig Bemelmans also have been featured on its pages.

Social commentary is a necessary part of our cultural pattern. We need to "see ourselves as others see us," and the cartoon holds up the mirror to society.

Definitions of art are many and varied. Winston's basic definition is an inclusive one: "The application of skill and taste to the production of beautiful things; the adaptation of things, by change or combination, to the accomplishment of some end; a practical skill, facility, an application of skill, to bring about some desired result."

Certainly this extended definition applies to the cartoon. Skill is definitely incorporated. Taste is relative, but nevertheless is implied. Beauty in the broad sense is a definite goal of the cartoonist, if form and expression, pattern and design, and message and aesthetics are considered. Most certainly the "adaptation of things by change or combination to the accomplishment of an end" (the bringing about of a desired result) would be almost a definition of cartooning itself.

Noted critic Paul G. Konody gives his definition of art: "In the modern and more restricted sense the term art applies only to those human activities which tend toward an aestheticism—in other words, the Fine Arts. . . ."

The cartoonist works exclusively in the field of human activities. He penetrates the outward man and reveals the inward man. He deals with *man,* not only the individual man, but the *Universal Man*—the "Adam symbol." If it is in the comic field, he uncovers man's weaknesses and foibles and humorously portrays them; if in the editorial field (the political cartoon), he satirizes the political man and his efforts to control himself and his environment; and if in the social or situation cartoon, the artist delves into the psychological man and his motivations. He expresses all of these purposefully and aesthetically. Konody also advised: "Art is not representation but interpretation; and it is not too much to say that art begins where the artist departs from strict imitation of nature, imposing upon her a rhythm of his own creation, according to his own sense of fitness."

What a concise picture of the cartoonist's art!

In the past the cartoon has had the stigma of being "non-intellectual," "low" in scope and nature, and too "plebeian" for an art form. Let us not forget, however, what I. G. Mattingly so pertinently observed in *Harpers Magazine:*

> It may almost be set down as a law of cultural history that the vulgar amusements of today are the highbrow art of tomorrow. The epic, the Italian opera, the Elizabethan drama—all were regarded at one time as entertainment of a rather low order, until at length the critics came to their rescue by proving that these things *were* art and thenceforth to be taken seriously.

In Europe, artists utilizing the cartoon—such as Daumier, Goya, Hogarth, Toulouse-Lautrec, and others—won wide recognition in the world of art. In our own country, some of the foremost artists were once newspaper artists or cartoonists. George Luks drew *The Yellow Kid.* Walt Kuhn was a panel cartoonist, Lyonel Feininger did a Sunday comic entitled *Your Uncle Feininger,* and the list is an endless one . . . Frederick Remington, Charles Russell, George Bellows, William Glackens, Everett Shinn, John Sloan, Reginald Marsh, Peggy Bacon, William Gropper, Boardman Robinson, Denys Wortman, John Groth, Howard Baer. . . .

Today the work of cartoonists adorns the great museums around the world. In the comic world, Walt Disney originals hang in the Metropolitan Museum of Art, the Museum of Modern Art, the Cleveland Museum of Art, the Toledo Museum of Art, the William Rockhill Nelson Gallery, the Phillips Collection, the San Francisco Museum of Art, and numerous foreign galleries. Such artists as Al Capp, Hal Foster, Walt Kelly, H. T. Webster, George Herriman, Alex Raymond, James Montgomery Flagg, and Charles Dana Gibson have their work represented in major galleries.

Among the political cartoonists, Fitzpatrick is represented in the major galleries. So are Herblock, Bruce Russell, Arthur Szyk, Edmund Duffy, Rube Goldberg, James T. Berryman, Orr and Parrish, and countless others of equal ability. Caricaturist Al Hirschfeld is represented in the Metropolitan Museum and the Museum of Modern Art and in numerous galleries in this country and abroad. In the social cartoon, such men as Robert Osborn, Saul Steinberg, and Whitney Darrow, Jr., have exhibited in museums across the country.

Cartoon shows in major galleries and art museums around the world attest to the fact that the cartoon is now recognized as a leading art form.

Styles in cartooning are many and varied and have greatly enhanced the arts around them. George Herriman, Cliff Sterrett, and Winsor McCay experimented in abstract design and color, influencing some of our great modern painters. Picasso has said he was greatly influenced by the simplification and design of the American comic artists.

It is interesting to note that the history of art is closely intertwined with the cartoon art form. As Mattingly observed,

"The essential elements of the comic-strip form are all very old. The insides of the pyramids, the walls of Pompeiian dwellings, to say nothing of the Bayeux tapestry, are covered with pictorial narrative. Around a side door of Chartres Cathedral, the story of Creation is told in a series of miniature gargoyles. At the point in the story where God conceives of Man, God is shown with a sort of balloon above his head containing a small human figure—his "idea"—precisely the way a modern comic-strip artist would depict it. A similar analogy exists between the work of Peter Brueghel and Fisher's Sunday cartoon, *Right Around Home*: both artists allow a variety of adults, children, dogs, birds, fish—every link of the Great Chain of Being—to react characteristically to a central situation or theme."

Many maintain that the cartoon is an exaggeration, a repellent view of nature—in essence, a caricature. We know, however, that beauty is not only a static picture of a lovely sunset sinking over a colorful mountain range—it is more than this! Beauty also can be ugly, and at times grotesque. If in the end this ugliness or grotesqueness stirs us emotionally in essentially a beautiful way, then art—true art—is born. How much of the true art of the past was only "prettiness"? Very little, I would vouch to say. It goes much deeper, to the heart of the emotions and what is conveyed. Much of the so-called "masters" is an exaggeration by the artist for effect. Paul Konody, in *Britannica*, observed:

We learn to see beauty in a tree, in a mountain, and even in things which, before the artist had opened our eyes, left us cold or even repelled us. A toothless old hag becomes beautiful under Rembrandt's magic touch, because he saw his subject emotionally and taught us to see it in the same way. It is doubtful if anybody found anything but dinginess and "ugliness" in the mist and fog of the Thames-side in London before Whistler, by the work of his brush and the poetic imagery of his "Ten o'clock Lecture," invested the murky London atmosphere with permanent beauty.

And so it is with the cartoon. The cartoon is seldom "pretty," or "nice," or "complimentary," or "fawning." It scratches across the surface of life, whether the raw slums of the teeming city or the palatial mansion of the millionaire. It tells perhaps better than any medium what people are *really* like. It shows this characteristic to the masses, simply and quickly, with humor and devastating satire. It uncovers the inner man for all to see and lays bare his soul, like it or not. And the surprising thing about it all is that, in doing so, it achieves a beauty both in message and form.

People are moved by cartoons. They laugh at themselves. They are able to see the foolishness of their ways, and perhaps to benefit thereby. The politician sees a cartoon and the reaction is immediate. Boss Tweed, an early-day politician, said when he saw the cartoons of Thomas Nast: "Stop them damn pictures! I don't care so much what they write about me, my constituents can't read; but damn it, they can see pictures."

What was he worried about? He was worried because those "damn pictures" conveyed the message of what Tweed was *really* like . . . not the rich, outwardly powerful, philanthropic, generous Tweed, but the corrupt, ruthless, criminal Tweed, and he could not bear to see himself. The cartoon gets to the core of man and nature and in a minimum of lines; and there *is* a beauty in the process. How deft is the pen line of Al Hirschfeld in capturing what a person is *really* like and in such an artistic way. How impressive is the crayon stroke of a Fitzpatrick or Herblock in commenting upon our times with Daumier-like power. How devastating is the roving pen of a Steinberg whose very designs unveil reality. Is it art? Many noted critics think so. Ulbrich Troubetzkoy said,

> "Cartoons combine art and humor—broad or subtle, satirical or farcical—in a form singularly congenial to the American temperament. They satisfy at once our predilections for speed, directness, brevity, and force. The power of a pictorial lampoon lies in its unique quality of striking both the senses and intellect with compact immediacy and with the most unanswerable and devastating of weapons, which is laughter. The limitless potential—good or bad—of the cartoon is in this ability at the same moment to instruct and entertain."

Lee Negow, in *The Saturday Review of Literature,* asked,

> Can the comic strip be art? Are the intellectuals who cheer ".'Abner" out of line? My answer is that it is certainly art, like the cartoons of Daumier, the epigrams of Martial, and the children's records of George Kleinsinger. As Steinbeck points out, Capp's

way with language is as extravagantly vital as Mark Twain's.

Ignatius Mattingly advised,

> The work of King, Caniff, and Capp—to name only three of the best—is ample evidence that comic strips are a serious art demanding serious study. All the medium really needs now is a set of critics who will edit the classics, define the genres, catalogue the conceits, and elaborate the aesthetics.

William P. Steven commented, "Comics have been called a good many things lately. Actually, the American comic is an art form. It may prove to be the most significant art form developed in America."

The answer has to be a strong, affirmative— YES!

The purpose of art is both to convey beauty and at the same time to communicate. What more effective way of communicating is there than the cartoon?

Joseph Musial, in a 1953 speech, observed,

> G. B. Shaw's nearly lifelong efforts to establish a phonetic alphabet were made not with tongue-in-cheek and not only to simplify English spelling, but to develop and promote a universal language. A form of communication older than language, very often more effective, and certainly universal in scope, is the cartoon. The successful cartoon reaches people because of its condensed form. Yet though physically static, it suggests movement, evokes hordes of other images, and tells a story. It tells not of a man but of men; not of a wedding or picnic, or a fear or an appetite, but of weddings, picnics, fears, and appetites *in general.* The cartoon hits home because its topic and situation are grasped at once by all who view it. Unlike literal illustrations, the cartoon employs exaggerated measurements, actions, and values. It not only presents truth, but also transforms universal, recognizable, appreciable truth into universal appeal.

The cartoon has one of the widest audiences of any art form in history. Statistics show that day in and day out over one hundred million people read the comics in this country alone. They are also immensely popular abroad and appear in almost every country, including the Soviet Union. Editorial cartoons can be seen regularly in the 1,730 U.S. dailies and many of the 7,626 weeklies. They also are popular in the other nations of the world. This numerical compilation does not include the cartoon material which appears in the periodicals and magazines around the country, nor does it include the animated cartoon and its worldwide appeal. A quick perusal of these figures shows at once the power of the "lowly" cartoon. It is without question the most popular art form in existence.

The cartoon's tremendous appeal to the common man has its base in the very nature of the cartoon itself, an instantaneous impact coupled with humorous and aesthetic components. It has an equal appeal to the young person and adult alike.

The cartoon comments succinctly upon our times. It mirrors our epoch. It preserves the national scene, its passing traits, and its customs. It does not compromise, but in the best tradition of the great artists of the past has the courage to humorously and at times powerfully attack the injustices of our times. Of all art forms, it is perhaps the most effective interpreter of our times, our heritage, our culture, and the spiritual concept or soul of the people.

Art's highest function is to reveal essential truths. The cartoonist penetrates to the heart of life, recreating the joy, the agony, and the significance of our existence—a seeing and relating that is the unique endeavor of man.

Postscript

aRt wOOD

IF THE CARTOON is indeed an art form, and perhaps the most popular one worldwide, then it deserves to be preserved, studied, and enjoyed.

Cults of enthusiastic young people have sprung up in America and abroad meeting in cities coast-to-coast to study the cartoon. These "ComiCons," as they are called, are mini-conventions attracting young and old alike. Collectors by the thousands are accumulating drawings, prints, cartoon books, old newspaper comic pages, and comic memorabilia. Some collect original political cartoons, and others gather original comic strips or special autographed sketches by comic artists. Others collect Disney artwork, cels, or letters and Christmas cards from cartoonists. Specialized publications are catering to this growing market. Even the Smithsonian Institution in Washington has published a number of cartoon anthologies to meet this increasing demand and has instituted a series of cartoon lectures in its associate program that have been popular and well-attended. Cartoons are the "new" American art, perhaps because of this widespread interest, or perhaps because they are available and affordable.

Fortunately, I began collecting original graphics as a young man and at a propitious time. Collecting original cartoons has been a labor of love and a lifetime avocation. Collecting drawings is a marvelous madness, an inflammation of the brain that infects every bone and fibre. It gives one a glazed look, a rhapsodic eye, and an iron determination to spread the malady everywhere. It is, however, a happy affliction requiring only time and perseverance to bring about a cure.

From humble beginnings, my collection has now reached sizeable proportions. More than twenty-five hundred artists are represented with perhaps thirty to forty thousand original drawings. My collection encompasses the entire graphic field—illustration, political cartoons, caricature, the comic strip, humorous or "gag" cartoons, and animation—making it the largest private collection of its kind in the world.

It is gratifying that cartoon art is finding its way into the major museums and galleries. This is the way it should be, and one day perhaps a Herriman original will hang side by side with a Picasso and a Windsor McCay with a Rubens.

What will become of this vast accumulation of American art? It has been my desire since I was a youngster to establish a National Center of the Cartoon Arts in the nation's capital. My dream is close to being realized.

Index

Cartoon Index

To: Dick Craig:—

My best wishes,
Dick, and tell that
outfit over at Penn
State, "Hello."
My best,

Norm Childers
4/15/74

This is a group of graduate students at Rutgers University in a fruit breeding class taught by Dr. L. Fredric Hough (third from left). These students are working toward masters and doctorate degrees in horticulture and come from Brazil, Scotland, Lebanon, Poland, Puerto Rico, Germany, Guatamala and Yugoslavia, aside from those from USA. Many of these special trained students are and will be World leaders and researchers in the fruit industry.

This book is dedicated to
THE YOUNG PEOPLE OF TODAY
Who will be the leaders of
the fruit industry tomorrow

Modern Fruit Science

Modern Fruit Science

Orchard and Small Fruit Culture

NORMAN FRANKLIN CHILDERS

M. A. Blake Professor and Research Specialist of Horticulture
Rutgers University — The State University of New Jersey, New Brunswick
Formerly Assistant Director and Senior Plant Physiologist
United States Department of Agriculture Experimental Station in Puerto Rico
Associate in Horticulture, Ohio Agricultural Experiment Station
Assistant Professor in Horticulture, The Ohio State University
Instructor, Cornell University

PLEASE ORDER ADDITIONAL BOOKS FROM:

HORTICULTURAL PUBLICATIONS
Rutgers University—The State University, Nichol Avenue
New Brunswick, New Jersey, 08903

Courtesy F. Hilkenbaumer, Institut Fur Obstbau der Universitat der Bonn, Germany.

This is a deciduous fruit growing region in West Germany. Vineyards are contoured on the river bank. Fruit trees on the level area are largely on EM and MM dwarfing stocks.

Courtesy Blue Star Growers, Inc., and Paul Stark, Jr., nurseryman-grower, Wapato, Washington.

This is a typical cooperative apple-pear packing and storage plant in the Wenatchee-Yakima deciduous tree fruit growing area of the Northwest, USA. This Blue Star Growers, Inc., plant at Cashmere has 70 members, 500,000 bu. cold storage, 100,000 bu. CA storage, and daily packing capacity of 7,500 bu. loose.

v

Printed by Somerset Press, Inc., Somerville, New Jersey
(Please order copies through Horticultural Publications,
Rutgers University, New Brunswick, New Jersey, 08903, U.S.A.)

Agricultural Photography by Grant Heilman, Lititz, Pa.

This is part of a 1000-acre orchard owned by John Peters and his four sons near Gardners, Pa. They grow mainly apples, peaches, and cherries with 50 acres of pears and plums. They have some plantings of dwarf Red and Golden Delicious and Red York trees. Pond stores pumped well water for irrigation of contoured orchard blocks at declining lower levels. Wooded areas are unsuited for fruit trees and modern machinery.

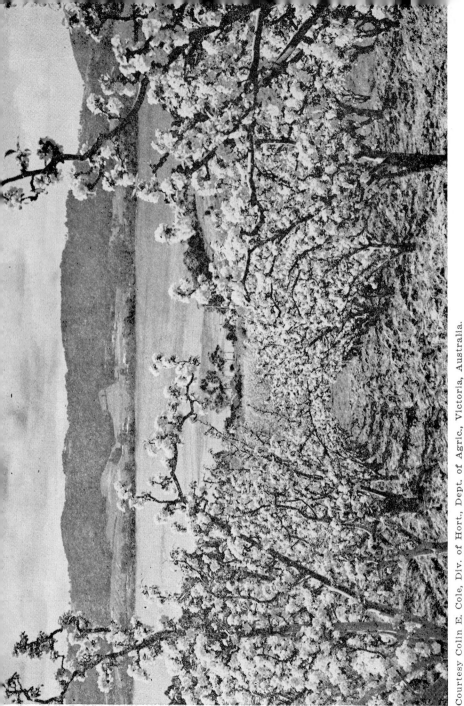

Courtesy Colin E. Cole, Div. of Hort., Dept. of Agric., Victoria, Australia.

This is a high-density apple orchard in bloom and on dwarfing stock in the Huon Valley, Tasmania. This is an important island of deciduous fruit growing off the southeast corner of Australia.

Preface

◆ ◆

This book has been prepared primarily for undergraduate *fruit and nut growing courses in colleges*. The author has made a special attempt, however, to make the book not only complete and technically accurate but interesting and easy-to-read so that it can be used as a text or reference in *vocational agriculture* and *short courses*. In addition, it is hoped that the book will be of value to the *grower* of fruits and nuts who believes that he has not mastered certain details of his business and who desires to keep abreast with trends and research developments.

While considerable information and research data are given in this text, it is left largely to the teacher to challenge his students with additional research data, theories, depth of discussion and assignments, depending upon their experience and scholastic level. A special effort has been made to present the subject material in an attractive logical manner, using numerous photographs and charts to keep the attention and interest of the reader so that he will not become bored and later fail to take active part in class discussions.

The subject matter presentation in this book is different from most fruit growing texts. The first two chapters are general and refer to all deciduous fruits to be discussed. The next few chapters are devoted to the apple since it is grown widely, and, being important, it has the most and best research background. The apple chapters cover in detail the important subjects from planting to marketing. Thus, the student has an opportunity to become acquainted with the scientific principles upon which the different practices in apple growing are based and with this foundation he should be able to understand and devise solutions for problems with other fruits. Actually, for all practical purposes, there are few basic differences among fruit and nut crops with regard to their growth processes, fruiting responses and cultural requirements.

A LABORATORY MANUAL for the MODERN FRUIT SCIENCE book is available, containing over 30 two- to three-hour exercises which supplement information given in this book. The MANUAL can be used 15 exercises in the basic course and about 15 exercises in the advanced pomology course. The MANUALS are available from the same source as the above book.

The remaining chapters in the tree-fruit section cover the management of other important temperate-zone fruits which are grown widely in the United States and many foreign countries. This section is followed by two general chapters covering pest control and fruit judging. Each of the important small fruits or groups of small fruits then is covered in a single chapter complete in itself.

The appendix has been broadened considerably to give the reader detail information that cannot be found in other books, such as a list of world publications carrying pomological information, cost-of-production data, and a list of books, nut nurseries and U.S. and Canadian experiment stations, and universities experimenting with and teaching deciduous fruits. The appendix also includes a glossary and an additional set of technical references on key subjects plus other pertinent information.

There is much variation in methods of teaching pomology and results obtained. The teacher's organization and *method of presentation* of material appear to be the most important factors governing student interest. Actually, the professor is probably more than 50 percent responsible for the success of his course; I often have thought 75 percent responsible. But the teacher obviously should not try to carry most of the weight; he must call upon and stimulate his students to contribute since by such an approach they will retain more information and generate more interest.

Each teacher has a personal pattern of presentation. The system which works well for one may make a poor showing for another. In the author's experience the above system of presenting a full picture of one fruit at a time seems to be less confusing to the student than when, for example, several pruning methods for a wide variety of fruits are jumbled together in one or two lectures. When such a discussion is concluded most students cannot seem to recall what practice is used on which fruit and why. If a student studies and thinks only one fruit from the time the varieties are selected until the product is sold, the entire picture unfolds as a story with a beginning and an end and experience seems to indicate that he retains more basic information about that fruit during and after the final examination.

The plan of presentation in this book also should lend itself to certain regions where some fruits are of little or no importance. For example, much less time would be devoted to cherries in Maine than in Michigan. The cranberry merely would be mentioned in Missouri whereas it is of outstanding importance in Massachusetts, Washington and Wisconsin. The subject matter is readily available to the fruit grower specializing in but one or two fruits. If a peach grower desires information on pruning, soil management, harvesting and other practices he finds it all in one chapter and thus it is not necessary for him to thumb through long general chapters on each orchard management phase to pick out those particular practices relating to the peach.

Pomology teachers should gradually build up a file of 2 x 2 color slides for each lecture and laboratory to break the monotony of straight lectures. An opaque projector is good to reflect bulletins and books, 8-½ x 11 inches or smaller, tables, pictures, and live material on the screen (Chas. Besler Co., Photo. Proj. Equip., E. Orange, N. J. Write for information.)

The portable-overhead-transparency projector with equipment to copy charts and tables on transparencies enables the teacher to operate the equipment on his desk in front of the class, pointing to numbers, bars on a graph, etc., and to draw diagrams while the class watches. The chart and pencil are reflected on a standard projection screen against the front wall. (Minnesota Mining and Manufacturing Co., Visual Products, 2501 Hudson Rd., St. Paul Minn. 55119.)

In the future, professors of pomology must increase their efforts as much as possible to attract promising young people to this field, for colleges and universities now are falling far short of meeting the needs for well-trained capable pomology graduates. It is hoped that this book will help the teacher in capturing at least a few more of the better students.

Professional men who reviewed and assisted in the chapters of the *first* to *third editions* were: Victor R. Gardner, John T. Bregger, Andrew E. Murneek, Melvin B. Hoffman, Louis J. Edgerton, H. A. Cardinell, M. T. Hilborn, Robert M. Smock, Archie Van Doren, Fred W. Burrows, Luther D. Davis, Frank P. Cullinan, A. M. Musser, L. L. Claypool, C. J. Hansen, Max McFee, William E. Young, Jr., W. H. Childs, Nelson J. Shaulis, George M. Darrow, W. P. Judkins, George L. Slate, and Paul L. Koenig. Also assisting were the *late* (in each case) David G. White, J. Lupton McCartney, Jr. K. Shaw, Karl D. Brase, J. H. Waring, Roy E. Marshall, D. F. Fisher, Leif Verner, Henry Hartman, Walter S. Hough, Frank H. Beach, I. C. Haut, Harold B. Tukey, Sr., and Stanley Johnston. Hayao Iwagaki, Japan, and S. A. Pieniazek, Poland, gave valuable help.

My colleagues at Rutgers University who assisted at the time of writing the first to third editions were: Carter R. Smith, L. Fredric Hough, Warren C. Stiles, Catherine H. Bailey, James N. Moore, Ernest G. Christ, Abdul Kamali, Laszlo Somogyi, A. B. Wills, Udar Mahal, Miklos Faust, W. B. Collins, M. W. Borys, W. J. Kender, and Mrs. Vera DeHart.

Professional workers who assisted in the revision of the chapters or parts of chapters of the *fourth* and *fifth editions* are given in the footnotes in the respective chapters. Others were William G. Doe, grower and representative of Marwald, Inc., Ayer Rd., Harvard, Mass. and Paul Stark, Jr. of Stark Nurseries and Orchards Co., Louisiana, Missouri both of whom gave considerable advice and help on a number of chapters, based on their background of wide experience. The late H. B. Tukey, Sr. of Michigan acted in a similar manner. Other professional state or federal people who assisted in one way or another and to whom I am grateful were R. Paul Larsen, Washington; James A. Beutel, California; Ewell A. Rogers, Colorado; Cecil Stushnoff, Minnesota; Ronald B. Tukey and Robert A. Norton, Washington; Donald V. Fisher and James Marshall, British Columbia; Chesley Smith, New Brunswick, Canada; George M. Kessler, Jordan Levin, H. P. Gaston, R. F. Carlson and A. L. Kenworthy, Michigan; Robert G. Hill, Jr., Ohio; Roy K. Simons and C. C. Zych, Illinois; Frank H. Emerson, Purdue; Hollis H. Bowen, Texas; Earl F. Savage, Georgia; David W. Buchanan and L. Gene Albrigo, Florida; Walter E. Ballinger and Gene J. Galletta, North Carolina; Ray S. Marsh, West Virginia; Hubert C. Mohr, Kentucky; Aubrey D. Hibbard and Delbert D. Hemphill, Mo., Justin R. Morris and A. A. Kattan, Arkansas; the late B. A. Dominick, Jr., Cornell; Lloyd A. Mitterling, Connecticut; F. W. Southwick, Massachusetts; V. G. Shutak, Rhode Island; W. J. Kender, New York; and my colleagues at Rutgers: Ernest G. Christ, Catherine H. Bailey, L. Fredric Hough and Paul Eck. Mrs. Karen Heller, my secretary for the Fifth Edition, did most of the typing. C. Palmer Bateman, Sr. and Jr., Ollie Welsh, and Artie Clark all have been very cooperative over the years in publishing the several editions of this and other horticultural books, manuals and related materials. All of these people gave more of their help than I probably should have accepted.

My wife, Lillian Coyne Childers, gave me considerable help and encouragement which I very much appreciate.

January 1973   Norman F. Childers

NOTE: The following are the "Ten Commandments for a Good Teacher" by Victor H. Wohlford in Better Farming Methods, October 1958: (1). PREPARE YOUR LESSON WELL. A lack of proper preparation is the unpardonable sin of a teacher. Nothing will inspire the confidence of his class so quickly as the teacher who makes adequate preparation of his lesson. (2). BE PRESENT WHENEVER POSSIBLE. Unnecessary absences will not teach your students to be punctual in their attendance, and will hinder interest and progress in your class. When it is necessary to be absent, always advise your substitute in sufficient time for him to make necessary preparation. (3). BE ON TIME. Negligence and indifference on the part of the teacher will soon be absorbed by the class. Be present several minutes before the time set for the class to begin. (4). BE PERSONALLY INTERESTED IN EACH MEMBER OF YOUR CLASS. Call members by their names. Be interested in the limitations and problems of each member of your class, and willingly give such attention or assistance to those problems as you can. (5). BE ATTENTIVE OF THE PHYSICAL CONDITIONS OF YOUR CLASSROOM. Before beginning the lesson, make necessary adjustment of the lights, ventilation, window shades, seating arrangements, maps, charts, blackboard, etc. (6). BEGIN AND CLOSE PROMPTLY. Do not wait for late comers, and do not extend the lesson beyond the time set to end the class. A violation of either of these points will distract interest from your class. Your promptness will beget promptness in your pupils. (7). DO NOT DO ALL THE TALKING. Do not make your lesson a lecture, as it takes a near genius to give an interesting lecture. Encourage class discussion. Never tell anything you can get your class to tell. (8). DO NOT PERMIT ARGUMENTS IN YOUR CLASS. Nothing will kill interest more quickly. Permit discussions of differences, but when they turn into arguments, pass on to the next question or point of discussion. (9). REALIZE YOUR SERIOUS RESPONSIBILITIES. Be as serious as possible about your teaching. Realize that what and how you teach may lead your pupils to fuller understanding and appreciation, or discourage their acceptance of the facts presented. (10). BE INTERESTED IN YOUR CLASS. Consider your students, and be wise in your teaching. A good slogan for teachers is: "If the student hasn't learned—the teacher hasn't taught."

—*Victor H. Wohlford*

Upper, Courtesy Don Curlee, Western Fruit Grower; lower, Paul Stark Jr., Stark Nurseries and Orchard Co., Louisiana, Missouri. 63353.

(Upper) In the Wenatchee-Yakima fruit growing region of Washington, USA, most of the orchards are located along river bottom land or low plateau areas near water. This is east of the Cascade Mountains and on the Columbia River from which much of the irrigation water comes. High sunlight, adequate water, and cool nights near harvest aid in the production of the highest quality fruit.

(Lower) This scene in the Yakima area shows pears in the background, sweet cherries in the center and spur Golden and Red Delicious in the foreground and at right.

Courtesy S. A. Pieniazek, Institute of Pomology, Skierniewice, Poland.

Origin of many of our cultivated fruits was in China over 4000 years ago. Commercial fruit growing in China began in earnest in 1949, the Chinese Revolutionary Victory year. This is an apple orchard on Malus baccata seedlings in Liaoning Province in eastern China, interplanted with peanuts. The Chinese were the first to use contour orchard planting.

U. S. Library of Congress
Catalogue Card No. 68-63552